Apress Pocket Guides

Apress Pocket Guides present concise summaries of cutting-edge developments and working practices throughout the tech industry. Shorter in length, books in this series aims to deliver quick-to-read guides that are easy to absorb, perfect for the time-poor professional.

This series covers the full spectrum of topics relevant to the modern industry, from security, AI, machine learning, cloud computing, web development, product design, to programming techniques and business topics too.

Typical topics might include:

- A concise guide to a particular topic, method, function or framework

- Professional best practices and industry trends

- A snapshot of a hot or emerging topic

- Industry case studies

- Concise presentations of core concepts suited for students and those interested in entering the tech industry

- Short reference guides outlining 'need-to-know' concepts and practices.

More information about this series at `https://link.springer.com/bookseries/17385`.

Industrial Control System (ICS) and Operational Technology (OT) Security

An Introduction to Securing a Complex Industrial Environment

Massimo Nardone

Apress®

Industrial Control System (ICS) and Operational Technology (OT) Security: An Introduction to Securing a Complex Industrial Environment

Massimo Nardone
Helsinki, Finland

ISBN-13 (pbk): 979-8-8688-2015-1   ISBN-13 (electronic): 979-8-8688-2016-8
https://doi.org/10.1007/979-8-8688-2016-8

Copyright © 2025 by Massimo Nardone

This work is subject to copyright. All rights are reserved by the Publisher, whether the whole or part of the material is concerned, specifically the rights of translation, reprinting, reuse of illustrations, recitation, broadcasting, reproduction on microfilms or in any other physical way, and transmission or information storage and retrieval, electronic adaptation, computer software, or by similar or dissimilar methodology now known or hereafter developed.

Trademarked names, logos, and images may appear in this book. Rather than use a trademark symbol with every occurrence of a trademarked name, logo, or image we use the names, logos, and images only in an editorial fashion and to the benefit of the trademark owner, with no intention of infringement of the trademark.

The use in this publication of trade names, trademarks, service marks, and similar terms, even if they are not identified as such, is not to be taken as an expression of opinion as to whether or not they are subject to proprietary rights.

While the advice and information in this book are believed to be true and accurate at the date of publication, neither the authors nor the editors nor the publisher can accept any legal responsibility for any errors or omissions that may be made. The publisher makes no warranty, express or implied, with respect to the material contained herein.

    Managing Director, Apress Media LLC: Welmoed Spahr
    Acquisitions Editor: Susan McDermott
    Development Editor: Laura Berendson
    Project Manager: Jessica Vakili

Distributed to the book trade worldwide by Springer Science+Business Media New York, 1 New York Plaza, New York, NY 10004. Phone 1-800-SPRINGER, fax (201) 348-4505, e-mail orders-ny@springer-sbm.com, or visit www.springeronline.com. Apress Media, LLC is a Delaware LLC and the sole member (owner) is Springer Science + Business Media Finance Inc (SSBM Finance Inc). SSBM Finance Inc is a **Delaware** corporation.

For information on translations, please e-mail booktranslations@springernature.com; for reprint, paperback, or audio rights, please e-mail bookpermissions@springernature.com.

Apress titles may be purchased in bulk for academic, corporate, or promotional use. eBook versions and licenses are also available for most titles. For more information, reference our Print and eBook Bulk Sales web page at http://www.apress.com/bulk-sales.

Any source code or other supplementary material referenced by the author in this book is available to readers on the Github repository: https://github.com/Apress/Industrial-Control-System-and Operational-Technology-Security. For more detailed information, please visit https://www.apress.com/gp/services/source-code.

If disposing of this product, please recycle the paper

Table of Contents

About the Author ix

Chapter 1: Introduction of Operational Technology (OT) Security and Industrial Control Systems (ICS) 1

Introduction and Definitions 2
Introduction of OT 4
OT Key Components 5
Typical OT Landscapes 7
Industries and Sectors Using OT 8
Difference Between IT and OT Environments 10
Why OT Security Is Needed, and What Are the Major and Common Cybersecurity Challenges That Demand Robust OT Security? 14
OT Security Market Trends 17
OT Security and Zero Trust Architecture 19
OT Security: Regulations, Standards, and Compliance 20
Introduction of IT–OT Convergence 21
IT–OT Convergence = Industrial Internet of Things (IIoT) 21
IT–OT Convergence: Cybersecurity Best Practices 23
Introduction of ICS 24
ICS Historical Background 27
Why ICS Matters? 28

TABLE OF CONTENTS

    Key Components of ICS 28

    OT and ICS Key Vendors 30

    Summary...33

Chapter 2: Key Components of Industrial Control Systems (ICS) 35

    Introduction of SCADA in Its Role in Industrial Operations.................37

        What Are the Unique Security Challenges in SCADA Systems?......41

    Introduction of Distributed Control System (DCS) 41

    Differences Between DCS and ICS...45

    Introduction of Programmable Logic Controller (PLC).........................47

    Introduction of Remote Terminal Units (RTUs) 50

    Human-Machine Interface (HMI) 53

    Introduction of ICS Controllers and Sensors 57

        What Are Sensors in ICS? 57

        What Are ICS Controllers? 58

    Summary...62

Chapter 3: Challenges and Cybersecurity Attacks in Operational Technology (OT) and Industrial Control Systems (ICS) 65

    The Growing Cyber Threat to Industrial Operations 66

    Why Is the ICS Environment Considered Challenging? 69

    OT Security Problems to Be Solved..72

    Introduction of Cybersecurity Attack in OT/ICS Environment..............79

        A Brief History of Cybersecurity Attacks on ICS 80

    Cybersecurity Threats and Incidents in ICS in 2022–2025 81

    Top ICS/OT Cybersecurity Threats in 2025 85

        Emerging Technologies in ICS and OT Cybersecurity 89

    Future of OT and ICS Cybersecurity 92

    Summary...95

Chapter 4: Operational Technology (OT) and Industrial Control Systems (ICS) Tools, Standards and Frameworks 97

Security Tools for ICS/OT 99

When Do We Need to Use a PAM (Privileged Access Management) Solution in an OT (Operational Technology) Environment?............................104

OT Security Protocols 106

OT Security Standards 108

Why Do Security Standards Matter? 109

ICS and OT Security Frameworks 115

Introduction of Standards and Technology (NIST) Cybersecurity Framework (CSF) 117

Purdue Enterprise Reference Architecture (PERA) 2.0 121

ICS and OT Security Regulations and Directives 126

Why Regulations and Directives Matter for OT Security? 127

How to Integrate Regulations and Directives? 130

Center Internet Security (CIS) 20 for ICS and OT 130

Critical Security Controls for ICS and OT 132

Summary 133

About the Author

Massimo Nardone has more than 30 years of experience in information and cybersecurity for IT/OT/IoT/IIoT, web/mobile development, cloud, and IT architecture. His true IT passions are security and Android. He holds an M.Sc. degree in computing science from the University of Salerno, Italy.

Throughout his working career, he has held various positions starting as Programming Developer, then Security Teacher, PCI QSA, Auditor, Assessor, Lead IT/OT/SCADA/Cloud Architect, CISO, BISO, Executive, Program Director, OT/IoT/IIoT Security Competence Leader, etc. In his last working engagement, he worked as a seasoned Cyber and Information Security Executive, CISO, and OT, IoT, and IIoT Security Competence Leader, helping many clients to develop and implement Cyber, Information, OT, and IoT Security activities.

He is currently working as Vice President of OT Security for SSH Communications Security.

He is a co-author of numerous Apress books, including *Spring Security 6 Recipes, Secure RESTful APIs, Cybersecurity Threats and Attacks in the Gaming Industry, Pro Spring Security, Beginning EJB in Java EE 8, Pro JPA 2 in Java EE 8*, and *Pro Android Games*, and has reviewed more than 100 titles.

CHAPTER 1

Introduction of Operational Technology (OT) Security and Industrial Control Systems (ICS)

In a world increasingly driven by automation and interconnected devices, securing Industrial Control Systems (ICS) and Operational Technology (OT) has become paramount.
Operational Technology (OT) refers to hardware and software systems used to monitor, control, and manage industrial processes, infrastructure, and assets.

Industrial Control Systems (ICS) Security refers to the protection of industrial automation and control systems used in critical infrastructure, manufacturing, and various industries.

CHAPTER 1 INTRODUCTION OF OPERATIONAL TECHNOLOGY (OT) SECURITY AND INDUSTRIAL CONTROL SYSTEMS (ICS)

These systems form the backbone of critical infrastructure industries such as energy, manufacturing, transportation, and water management. They enable everything from the management of electric grids to the automation of production lines, making their resilience a cornerstone of modern society.

With the convergence of IT and OT environments, security challenges have multiplied. ICS and OT systems, once isolated, are now often connected to corporate networks and the Internet, exposing them to a new array of cyber threats. Attacks on these systems can lead to catastrophic outcomes, including operational disruption, physical damages, financial losses, and threats to human safety.

This new pocketbook delves into the essential strategies, technologies, tools, standards, frameworks, and best practices for securing ICS and OT environments. It provides a comprehensive guide to understanding the unique security requirements of these systems, the evolving threat landscape, and the methods to protect critical infrastructure from potential cyber-attacks. From securing communication protocols to employing advanced threat detection, this book offers essential insights for safeguarding the heart of modern industrial operations.

In this chapter, we will start by introducing what are ICS and OT and how they differentiate from IT.

Introduction and Definitions

First, let's introduce the major technologies and some of the differences.

- **Information technology (IT)** is the use of computers to store, retrieve, transmit, and manipulate data, or information, often in the context of a business or other enterprise.

CHAPTER 1   INTRODUCTION OF OPERATIONAL TECHNOLOGY (OT) SECURITY AND INDUSTRIAL CONTROL SYSTEMS (ICS)

- **Consumer Technology (CT)** is hardware and software utilized by the end user (e.g., homes, phone apps, etc.).

- **Operational Technology (OT)** is hardware and software that detects or causes a change through the direct monitoring and/or control of physical devices such as valves, pumps, temperature sensors, gas sensors, etc., within industrial processes.

- **The Internet of Things (IoT)** is the network of physical devices, vehicles, appliances, and other items embedded with electronics, software, sensors, actuators, and connectivity that enables these things to connect and exchange data.

- **Industrial IoT (IIoT)** is a subset of IoT.

    IIoT are IoT systems that connect and integrate industrial control systems with enterprise systems, business processes, and analytics. (Industrial Internet Consortium Definition)

The technologies and how they interlink to each other are shown in Figure 1-1.

CHAPTER 1 INTRODUCTION OF OPERATIONAL TECHNOLOGY (OT) SECURITY AND INDUSTRIAL CONTROL SYSTEMS (ICS)

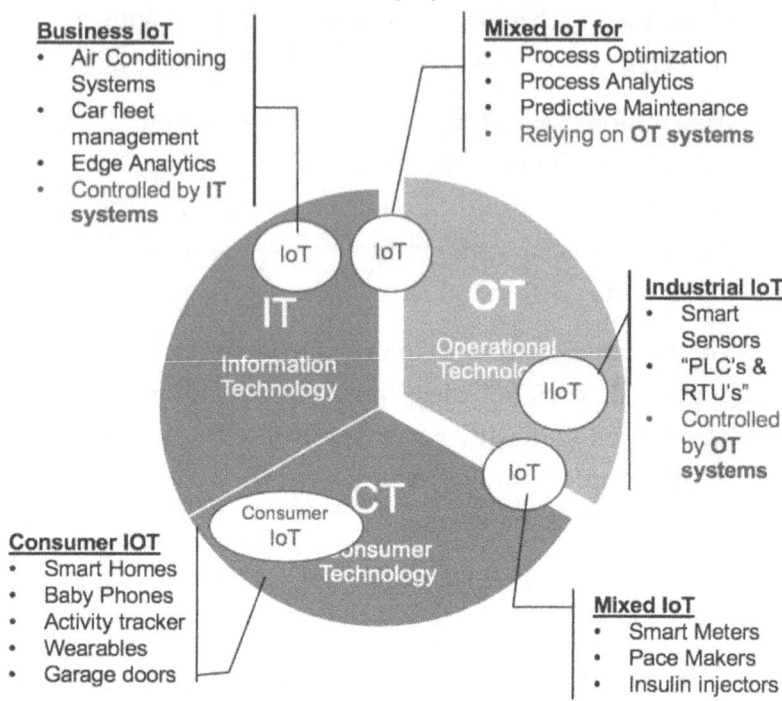

Figure 1-1. Introduction of technologies

Introduction of OT

Operational Technology (OT) refers to hardware and software that detects or causes changes through direct monitoring and control of physical devices, processes, and events within an enterprise.

Historically, OT systems were isolated and designed with minimal concern for cyber threats. However, the increasing integration of OT with IT networks, the advent of IoT (Internet of Things), and the rising sophistication of cyber threats have shifted the landscape dramatically. Today, safeguarding these systems requires new strategies and solutions tailored to their unique vulnerabilities.

CHAPTER 1   INTRODUCTION OF OPERATIONAL TECHNOLOGY (OT) SECURITY AND INDUSTRIAL CONTROL SYSTEMS (ICS)

Unlike IT, where the primary goals are confidentiality and accessibility, OT security emphasizes safety and reliability. Implementing effective OT cybersecurity involves using specialized software to monitor, analyze, and manage industrial systems and machinery, whether on-site or remotely. This software enables centralized access to all operational hardware, giving OT teams a comprehensive, real-time view of their entire infrastructure—from the endpoint devices to the control systems. Such visibility allows for rapid detection and resolution of anomalies, ideally before they cause significant damage or downtime.

OT security has become a critical necessity, particularly with the rise of the Internet of Things (IoT). IoT facilitates seamless communication between devices, delivering the convenience and efficiency demanded by modern households and businesses alike. Many warehouses and manufacturing plants have upgraded their equipment with interoperable, Internet-connected capabilities to optimize operations—reducing the need for constant human oversight.

However, technological progress often introduces new vulnerabilities. As industrial systems adopt IoT, they inherit the cybersecurity risks associated with Internet-connected devices.

Traditional IT cybersecurity solutions, designed primarily for data confidentiality and user access, are often insufficient for protecting OT interfaces and systems, which require tailored security measures to address their unique operational demands.

OT Key Components

Within the Operational Technology (OT) sector, the **Industrial Control Systems (ICS)** is a major segment. ICS comprises systems that are used to monitor and control industrial processes like oil refinery cracking towers, power consumption on electricity grids, or alarms from building information systems.

CHAPTER 1 INTRODUCTION OF OPERATIONAL TECHNOLOGY (OT) SECURITY AND INDUSTRIAL CONTROL SYSTEMS (ICS)

ICS may consist of the following:

- **SCADA:** Supervisory Control And Data Acquisition system, which is a combination of hardware and software that enables the automation of industrial processes by capturing Operational Technology (OT) real-time data.

- **DCS:** Distributed Control Systems, which is a digital automated industrial control system (ICS) that uses geographically distributed control loops throughout a factory, machine, or control area.

- **PLC:** Programmable Logic Controller, which is an industrial computer control system that continuously monitors the state of input devices and makes decisions based upon a custom program to control the state of output devices.

- **HMI:** Human Machine Interfaces, which is the hardware or software through which an operator interacts with a controller.

- **Controllers:** Controllers are component of ICS that maintain conformance with specifications.

- **Sensors:** Sensors are used to measure parameters, such as temperature, pressure, humidity, flow rate, and other vital industrial variables.

OT key components are shown in Figure 1-2.

CHAPTER 1   INTRODUCTION OF OPERATIONAL TECHNOLOGY (OT) SECURITY AND INDUSTRIAL CONTROL SYSTEMS (ICS)

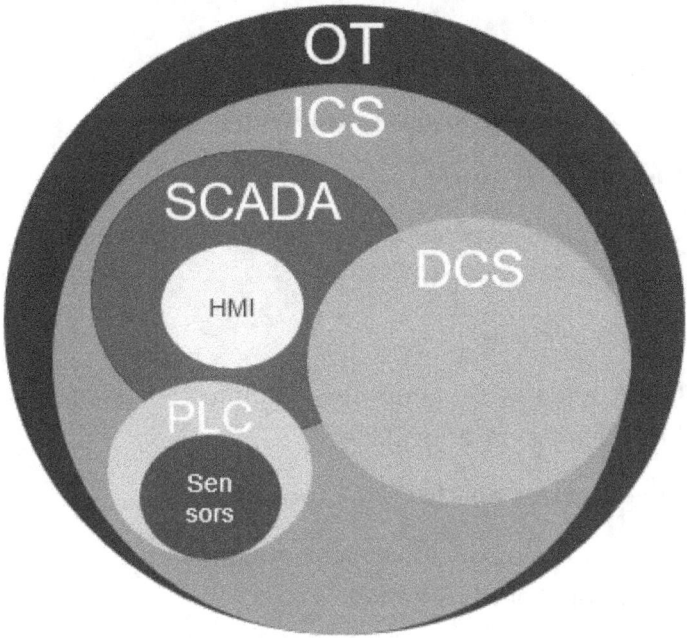

Figure 1-2. *OT Key Components*

Typical OT Landscapes

These landscapes include networks and systems used to **monitor, control, and automate** physical processes:

- **Industrial Control Systems (ICS)**

    SCADA, DCS, and PLCs used to control and monitor physical devices.

- **Manufacturing Execution Systems (MES)**

    Bridges operations and business systems, often linked to ERP.

- **Field Devices**

    Sensors, actuators, HMIs, and RTUs directly interacting with physical equipment.

- **Industrial Networks**

    Use specialized protocols like Modbus, Profibus, OPC-UA, Ethernet/IP.

- **Legacy Systems**

    Often outdated OS and software, difficult to patch, but still mission-critical.

- **Edge Devices and IoT/IIoT Gateways**

    Increasingly present to collect and transmit operational data securely.

Trends Impacting OT Landscapes include the following:

- **Convergence of IT and OT**
- **Rise of IoT and IIoT**
- **Increased regulatory scrutiny (NIS2, IEC 62443, etc.)**
- **Need for post-quantum and agentless secure access**
- **Cloud and edge computing integration**

Industries and Sectors Using OT

Here are listed the most common industries and sectors using OT:

1. **Energy and Utilities**
    - Power generation (nuclear, thermal, and hydro)
    - Smart grids and substations

CHAPTER 1   INTRODUCTION OF OPERATIONAL TECHNOLOGY (OT) SECURITY AND INDUSTRIAL CONTROL SYSTEMS (ICS)

- Oil and gas pipelines
- Water and wastewater management

2. **Manufacturing and Industrial Automation**

    - Automotive, electronics, and aerospace
    - Food and beverage processing
    - Pharmaceutical and chemical production

3. **Transportation and Logistics**

    - Rail systems (signal and control)
    - Airports and ports
    - Traffic management systems

4. **Critical Infrastructure**

    - Water treatment plants
    - Telecommunications infrastructure
    - Emergency services (public safety networks)

5. **Mining and Metals**

    - Remote operations control
    - Drilling and extraction systems
    - Conveyor and sorting automation

6. **Oil and Gas**

    - Refineries
    - Offshore platforms
    - SCADA in upstream/midstream

CHAPTER 1   INTRODUCTION OF OPERATIONAL TECHNOLOGY (OT) SECURITY AND INDUSTRIAL CONTROL SYSTEMS (ICS)

7. **Building Automation and Smart Infrastructure**

    - HVAC, elevators, and lighting control
    - Access control and video surveillance (also intersects with IoT)

8. **Healthcare (BioTech/MedTech OT)**

    - Clean room monitoring
    - Industrial sterilization
    - Infrastructure supporting labs and pharma plants

Difference Between IT and OT Environments

To fully understand the difference between IT and OT security, it's important to consider the motivations behind cyberattacks in each environment. In IT systems, attackers typically seek valuable data—personal, financial, or proprietary information—they can exploit for profit. In contrast, OT (Operational Technology) attacks are often aimed at causing physical disruption, targeting the machinery and processes that keep industrial operations running.

In OT environments, attackers frequently exploit unsecured IoT-enabled devices as entry points, gradually working their way toward critical control systems—often without needing login credentials. Consider a water bottling plant, for example. Its operations may include water collection, purification, and packaging. If OT security measures are lacking, a single compromised device in any of these stages could introduce contamination, potentially resulting in unsafe products reaching consumers. Such a breach could trigger serious health, legal, and economic repercussions before it's even detected.

CHAPTER 1   INTRODUCTION OF OPERATIONAL TECHNOLOGY (OT) SECURITY AND INDUSTRIAL CONTROL SYSTEMS (ICS)

In IT-centric enterprises, hackers typically go after credentials that allow access to servers storing confidential information. While this data theft can be highly damaging, IT attackers generally **do not have direct control over** physical systems or equipment—a capability that OT-based malware often possesses.

The core distinction is this:

- **IT security** focuses on **protecting data** and ensuring its confidentiality, integrity, and availability.

- **OT security**, on the other hand, is dedicated to **safeguarding physical assets**—including infrastructure, equipment, products, and even human lives.

A strong OT security solution is capable of automatically halting operations the moment abnormal behavior is detected in equipment, allowing time for investigation and remediation before the issue escalates. Because OT processes often follow a linear and observable sequence, anomalies are easier to detect and isolate. In contrast, IT breaches can go unnoticed for months, given the vast number of potential access points and the abstract nature of digital data movement.

While IT environments primarily focus on data confidentiality, integrity, and user access, OT environments prioritize safety, reliability, and availability of physical processes. Key differences include the following:

- **Goals:** OT aims to maintain operational continuity and physical safety, whereas IT emphasizes protecting data privacy.

- **System Nature:** OT systems often involve real-time control and are built on proprietary protocols, while IT systems are data-centric and standardized.

CHAPTER 1   INTRODUCTION OF OPERATIONAL TECHNOLOGY (OT) SECURITY AND INDUSTRIAL CONTROL SYSTEMS (ICS)

- **Downtime Tolerance:** OT systems are designed for high availability; even brief outages can cause significant safety hazards or economic losses.

- **Connectivity:** Traditionally isolated, OT networks are now increasingly interconnected with IT networks, exposing them to cyber threats.

OT Systems have many differences from traditional IT systems including the following:

- **Performance and reliability**: Real time; response time is critical; high delay or jitter is not acceptable.

- **Availability**: Responses as rebooting are not acceptable; availability is critical; so redundant systems are needed; outages are not acceptable; planned weeks in advance.

- **Risk management**: Controlling the physical world (environment, physical process) and human safety is paramount; fault tolerance is essential; even momentary downtime may not be acceptable.

- **Proprietary software or communication protocols**: Without security capabilities; difficult to make changes; sometimes vendors don't exist or support software anymore.

- **Component lifetime**: 10 or 15 years (IT 4 or 5).

Table 1-1 highlights the key differences between OT (Operational Technology) Security and IT (Information Technology) Security.

Table 1-1. *OT Security Comparison with IT Security*

Aspect	OT Security	IT Security
Primary Goals	Safety, reliability, availability	Confidentiality, integrity, and availability
Focus	Protecting physical systems and processes	Protecting digital data and information systems
System Nature	Real-time, embedded, industrial control systems	Data-driven, enterprise applications, cloud, and networks
Operations Priority	Ensuring continuous operation and safety	Protecting data confidentiality and preventing breaches
Downtime Tolerance	Very low; outages can cause safety risks or damage	Moderate; downtime is costly but often less directly dangerous
Response Approach	Rapid, often necessity-driven, with safety in mind	Usually policy-driven, with focus on incident response and forensics
Connectivity	Increasingly connected via IoT, but traditionally isolated	Generally connected to the broader enterprise, Internet, and cloud
Security Challenges	Legacy systems, real-time operational constraints, safety protocols	Data breaches, insider threats, malware, phishing attacks
Protection Focus	Industrial protocol security, physical device safety	User access control, data encryption, network security
Typical Threat Actors	State-sponsored, nation-states, industrial espionage	Cybercriminals, insiders, hacktivists
Impact of Breach	Physical damage, safety hazards, operational downtime	Data loss, financial fraud, reputation damage

CHAPTER 1 INTRODUCTION OF OPERATIONAL TECHNOLOGY (OT) SECURITY AND INDUSTRIAL CONTROL SYSTEMS (ICS)

This comparison underscores that OT security focuses heavily on physical safety, operational continuity, and reliability, while IT security emphasizes data confidentiality, privacy, and integrity—though both are increasingly interconnected and require specialized approaches.

Why OT Security Is Needed, and What Are the Major and Common Cybersecurity Challenges That Demand Robust OT Security?

Operational Technology (OT) security is vital for protecting critical infrastructure that sustains societal functions such as power generation, water supply, and transportation. Disruptions or cyberattacks on OT systems can result in the following:

- **Large-scale operational shutdowns**
- **Safety hazards for personnel and the environment**
- **Economic losses and production delays**
- **National security risks**

OT environments face unique cybersecurity threats that stem from both digital and physical entry points. One major vulnerability is the use of **external hardware**, such as USB flash drives or dongles. When these devices are shared across multiple machines or systems, they can easily transmit malware across connected networks. Each connection point increases the chance of infection, especially if the device has been compromised. To reduce this risk, it is best practice to **dedicate specific external hardware to designated networks**. Additionally, implementing **up-to-date antivirus software** offers an extra layer of defense when cross-network usage is unavoidable.

CHAPTER 1   INTRODUCTION OF OPERATIONAL TECHNOLOGY (OT) SECURITY AND INDUSTRIAL CONTROL SYSTEMS (ICS)

Another growing challenge involves the transition from traditional air-gapped OT systems to **IoT-connected infrastructure**. As organizations modernize their industrial environments, **cybersecurity professionals caution against underestimating the risk of improperly managed "air gaps."** These gaps—once physical barriers between IT and OT—can become gateways for exploitation if not addressed during the integration process. Ensuring secure data handling, storage, and network segmentation during this transition is essential. Once OT systems are online and connected, threats such as **bots and distributed denial-of-service (DDoS) attacks** become increasingly dangerous. These attacks can disrupt operations by overwhelming systems with traffic or disabling key control mechanisms.

Securing OT environments presents several challenges:

- **Legacy and Proprietary Protocols:** Many OT systems run on outdated, proprietary protocols that lack modern security features.

- **Real-Time Operations and Safety Constraints:** Security measures must not interfere with critical operations or cause downtime.

- **Limited Patch Management:** Many OT devices cannot be easily patched or updated without risking system instability.

- **Connectivity and Convergence:** Increased interconnection with enterprise networks elevates attack surfaces.

- **Resource Constraints:** OT systems often have limited processing capabilities, restricting the deployment of advanced security solutions.

CHAPTER 1 INTRODUCTION OF OPERATIONAL TECHNOLOGY (OT) SECURITY AND INDUSTRIAL CONTROL SYSTEMS (ICS)

However, even after describing all the technology challenges, the most persistent and unpredictable threat to OT security is **human error**. No matter how advanced a cybersecurity solution may be, it cannot fully protect against mistakes such as the following:

- **Irregular system monitoring**
- **Shared or weak credentials**
- **Inadequate emergency response protocols**
- **General carelessness or oversight**

Cybercriminals often exploit these human vulnerabilities, knowing that even minor lapses in protocol can open significant security gaps. To mitigate this, organizations must invest in ongoing employee training, reinforcing best practices in both IT and OT security. Regular awareness campaigns, drills, and policy reviews help maintain vigilance and ensure quick, informed responses to suspicious activity.

The major reasons why OT Security is needed are shown in Figure 1-3.

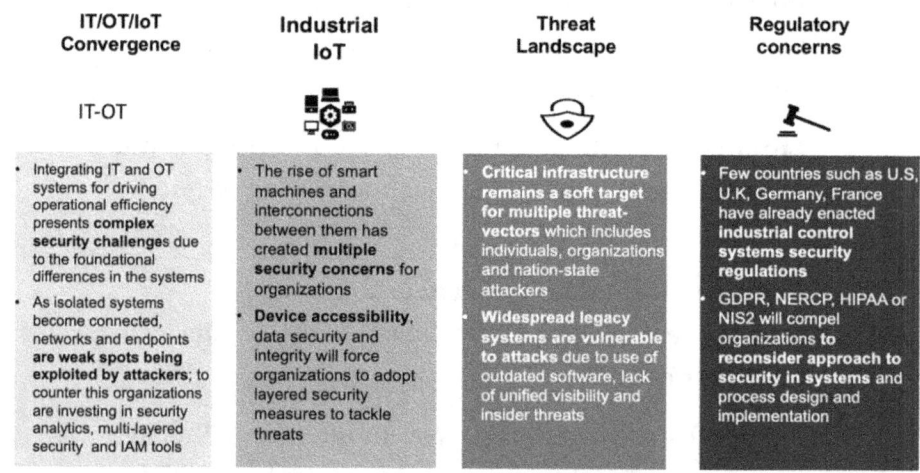

Figure 1-3. *Major reasons why Ot Security is needed*

CHAPTER 1 INTRODUCTION OF OPERATIONAL TECHNOLOGY (OT) SECURITY AND INDUSTRIAL CONTROL SYSTEMS (ICS)

OT Security Market Trends

Here is the list of the OT Security market trends (in 2025) based on Gartner, IoT Analytics, ENISA, NIST, and ISACA reports.

Major market trends:

- **Convergence of IT and OT Security:** With the increasing integration of IT and OT systems, there's a growing need for convergence in security strategies. Organizations are adopting unified approaches to security that bridge the gap between traditionally siloed IT and OT security teams. (our won OT Sec cases Stora Enso, Outokumpu, Konecranes dealing with IT/OT Convergence)

- **Zero Trust Architecture**: Zero Trust security models are gaining traction in OT environments. These models assume that threats could be both external and internal, and thus require continuous authentication and authorization for all users and devices, regardless of their location within the network.

- **Regulatory and Compliance**: Governments and industry regulators are placing greater emphasis on OT security compliance. New regulations and standards specific to OT security are being introduced to ensure the protection of critical infrastructure and industrial assets.

- **AI and Machine Learning**: AI and machine learning technologies are being leveraged to enhance OT security by analyzing vast amounts of data to identify patterns indicative of cyber threats or anomalies in operational processes.

Also to be considered are the following:

- **Incident Response and Resilience:** Given the potential impact of cyberattacks on OT systems, organizations are focusing on improving incident response capabilities and building resilience into their OT environments. This includes developing and testing response plans, establishing redundant systems, and implementing recovery strategies to minimize downtime and operational disruption.

- **Endpoint Protection:** As more OT devices become connected to networks, ensuring the security of endpoints is paramount. Endpoint protection solutions tailored for OT environments are emerging to provide real-time monitoring, threat detection, and response capabilities for industrial devices.

- **Cloud Adoption:** While cloud adoption in OT environments has been slower compared to IT, there's a growing trend toward leveraging cloud services for data storage, analytics, and management of OT systems. Secure cloud architectures specifically designed for OT are being developed to address the unique security requirements of industrial environments.

- **Supply Chain Security:** With the increasing interconnectedness of supply chains, ensuring the security of third-party vendors and suppliers is critical. Organizations are implementing supply chain risk management practices to assess and mitigate security risks associated with external partners.

- **Awareness and Training:** As the human element remains a significant factor in OT security, organizations are investing in employee training and awareness programs to educate personnel about the risks associated with cyber threats and best practices for maintaining a secure OT environment.

- **Integration of OT Security into Risk Management:** OT security is increasingly being integrated into broader enterprise risk management frameworks. Organizations are conducting comprehensive risk assessments that consider both cyber and physical threats to OT systems, enabling more informed decision-making and resource allocation to mitigate risks effectively.

OT Security and Zero Trust Architecture

The integration of Zero Trust Architecture (ZTA) into Operational Technology (OT) security is becoming increasingly critical as industries digitize and cyber threats evolve. Zero Trust is a security framework that assumes no implicit trust within or outside the network perimeter and requires continuous verification of every request as if it originates from an open network. Applying ZTA principles to OT environments involves several key components and strategies.

Key Components of Zero Trust Architecture in OT Security include the following:

- Identity and Access Management (IAM)
- Network Segmentation
- Monitoring and Analytics
- Device Security

CHAPTER 1   INTRODUCTION OF OPERATIONAL TECHNOLOGY (OT) SECURITY AND
INDUSTRIAL CONTROL SYSTEMS (ICS)

- Data Security
- Threat Detection and Response
- Policy Enforcement
- Assessing the Current State
- Defining the Zero Trust Scope
- Developing a Zero Trust Roadmap
- Enhancing Identity and Access Management
- Implementing Network Segmentation
- Deploying Advanced Monitoring and Analytics
- Strengthening Device and Data Security
- Developing and Enforcing Security Policies
- Continuous Improvement

OT Security: Regulations, Standards, and Compliance

Operational Technology (OT) environments, crucial for managing industrial operations and critical infrastructure, face increasing regulatory and compliance pressures to ensure their security.

Here are some of the key OT Security regulations, standards, and directives:

- NIST SP 800-82 (National Institute of Standards and Technology)
- NERC CIP (North American Electric Reliability Corporation Critical Infrastructure Protection)
- IEC 62443 (International Electrotechnical Commission)

- GDPR (General Data Protection Regulation)
- ISO/IEC 27001
- NIS2

More info about tools, standards, and framework will be discussed in Chapter 4.

Introduction of IT–OT Convergence

IT-OT convergence is crucial for driving efficiency, enhancing security, fostering collaboration, and leveraging data analytics, ultimately leading to a competitive advantage in today's fast-paced industrial landscape.

As organizations move toward digital transformation and Industry 4.0 initiatives, IT-OT convergence is essential to leverage technologies such as IoT, artificial intelligence, and big data, which require interoperability between IT and OT systems.

IT–OT Convergence = Industrial Internet of Things (IIoT)

IT-OT convergence is basically integration of People, Process, and Technology (PPT), requiring the following:

- A Governance Structure to determine how does the organization move about solving cyber challenges
- Tools Implementation that enables monitoring, measuring, and managing the cyber security threats
- Managed security portfolio that does continuous monitoring
- An awareness program, which provides continuous awareness to the users

CHAPTER 1 INTRODUCTION OF OPERATIONAL TECHNOLOGY (OT) SECURITY AND INDUSTRIAL CONTROL SYSTEMS (ICS)

Key challenges in the IT-OT convergence are shown in Figure 1-4.

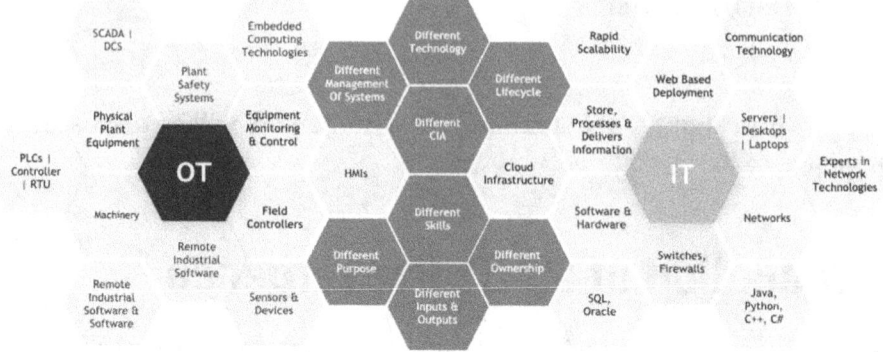

Figure 1-4. *Key challenges in the IT-OT convergence*

When combining IT and OT Security and adding Zero Trust and Quantum Safe Encryption, the results are shown in Figure 1-5.

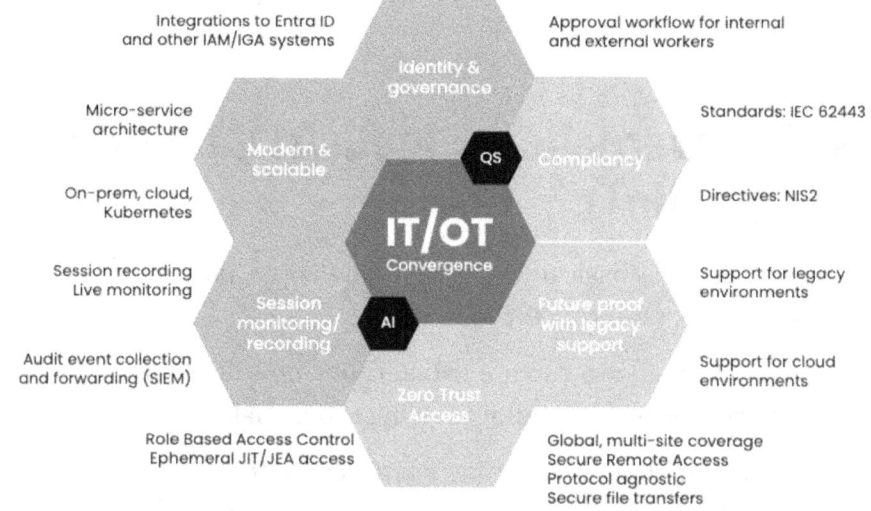

Figure 1-5. *Combining IT-OT differences*

IT–OT Convergence: Cybersecurity Best Practices

Below are listed the most important IT–OT Convergence Cybersecurity best practices.

- The **vision, strategy, and execution of the business plan** need to include security, reliability and safety. These should be part of the business planning process at all levels of the organization (regardless if you are an IoT solution provider or a customer).

- **Security should be "owned"** by one person at the executive level who is responsible for both IT and operations. Security policy, governance, and end-user education need to extend across the IT and OT environments as systems are interconnected.

- Technologies and threats across the IT and OT environments **should be clearly understood**. Technologies that work in the IT environment may not necessarily work in the OT environment. Additionally, threats may be different in the IT and OT environments.

- **A threat intelligence framework** needs to be set up so that the organization can be up-to-date on the latest information on threats and be prepared to deal with them.

- **Baseline security controls** should be deployed across all layers of the organization's environments.

- Regular risk assessments across all environments must be performed to identify vulnerabilities and ensure that the appropriate security controls are in place.

CHAPTER 1   INTRODUCTION OF OPERATIONAL TECHNOLOGY (OT) SECURITY AND
            INDUSTRIAL CONTROL SYSTEMS (ICS)

- The organization and customers should consider **NIST 800-5310 for IT and NIST 800-8211 and ISA/IEC 6244312** for ICS and OT.

- Establish or update the security patch process to better address vulnerabilities. Follow the recommendations laid out in IEC **62443-2-3**, which describes requirements for patch management for control systems.

- Develop **ICS-specific policies and procedures** that are consistent with IT security, physical safety, and business continuity.

Introduction of ICS

Industrial Control Systems (ICS) are a vital subset of **Operational Technology (OT)**, specifically designed to control, automate, and monitor industrial processes. Whether in manufacturing, power generation, or water treatment, ICS ensures that critical operations function efficiently, safely, and with minimal interruption.

ICS encompasses a range of technologies and systems that work together to manage complex industrial environments. These systems are essential for maintaining consistent production, optimizing performance, and responding to real-time operational demands.

The main differences between Industrial Control Systems (ICS) and Operational Technology (OT) are as follows:

Industrial Control Systems (ICS)

1. **Definition:**
   - Specifically refers to devices and software that control and automate physical processes within

CHAPTER 1 INTRODUCTION OF OPERATIONAL TECHNOLOGY (OT) SECURITY AND INDUSTRIAL CONTROL SYSTEMS (ICS)

industrial settings. Key components include SCADA, DCS, and PLCs.

2. **Functionality:**

   - ICS is primarily focused on the automation and precise control of industrial machinery and processes. They ensure continuous operation and efficiency.

3. **Components:**

   - **SCADA:** Used for remote monitoring and control by gathering data in real-time from various locations.
   - **DCS:** Controls processes across single or multiple locations with centralized control functions.
   - **PLCs:** Robust hardware used for a wide range of automation applications and responsive control.

4. **Applications:**

   - Used in manufacturing lines, power generation, water treatment, and other specific process control functions.

5. **Goals:**

   - Prioritizing operational continuity, precise control, and safety in automated processes.

Operational Technology (OT):

1. **Definition:**

   - Encompasses all technology used to monitor, control, and manage physical devices, processes, and infrastructure. Includes ICS as well as other

CHAPTER 1 INTRODUCTION OF OPERATIONAL TECHNOLOGY (OT) SECURITY AND INDUSTRIAL CONTROL SYSTEMS (ICS)

    systems and networks involved in industrial operations.

2. **Functionality:**

   - Broader than ICS, OT involves the oversight, management, and operational efficiency of entire industrial environments.

3. **Components:**

   - Includes sensors, actuators, control devices, communication networks, and security systems.
   - Integrates with business processes through IT technologies for decision-making and efficiency.

4. **Applications:**

   - Widespread across various industries like utilities, oil and gas, manufacturing, transportation, and smart buildings.

5. **Goals:**

   - Beyond control, OT ensures overall operational efficiency, safety, regulatory compliance, and integration with IT for enhanced data-driven strategies.

Key Differences:

- **Scope:**

CHAPTER 1 INTRODUCTION OF OPERATIONAL TECHNOLOGY (OT) SECURITY AND INDUSTRIAL CONTROL SYSTEMS (ICS)

- ICS focuses specifically on control systems, while OT includes ICS and other technologies for broader operational management.

- **Integration with IT:**

  - OT is increasingly integrated with IT for better analysis, control, and business continuity, whereas ICS traditionally functions independently focused on control and automation.

- **Security Needs:**

  - Both require rigorous security, but OT security must address a wider array of technologies and interconnected systems.

Understanding these distinctions helps highlight the roles each plays in industrial environments, and why tailored security and operational strategies are essential.

ICS Historical Background

The origins of ICS date back to the early 20th century with the introduction of mechanical relay-based control systems. However, the real evolution began in the 1960s and 70s with the invention of **Programmable Logic Controllers (PLCs)**, which replaced bulky and inflexible relay panels in industrial plants.

The 1980s and 90s saw the rise of **Distributed Control Systems (DCS)** and **Supervisory Control and Data Acquisition (SCADA)**, enabling centralized control over vast and complex operations. Over time, the integration of **digital communications**, **industrial networking**, and more recently, the **Industrial Internet of Things (IIoT)**, has transformed ICS into highly interconnected and intelligent ecosystems.

CHAPTER 1   INTRODUCTION OF OPERATIONAL TECHNOLOGY (OT) SECURITY AND
            INDUSTRIAL CONTROL SYSTEMS (ICS)

Why ICS Matters?

ICS is not just about automation—it's about ensuring **operational continuity**, **safety**, and **efficiency** in environments where downtime can have significant financial, safety, or environmental consequences. From manufacturing facilities to power plants, ICS enables precise control over equipment and processes, ensuring that operations run predictably and securely.

Whether you're managing a smart factory or a nationwide utility grid, **Industrial Control Systems are the backbone of modern industrial infrastructure**, delivering the control and visibility needed to support mission-critical activities.

Key Components of ICS

The effectiveness of ICS lies in its integrated components, each serving a unique function in automating and controlling industrial systems:

- **Programmable Logic Controllers (PLCs):** PLCs are specialized industrial computers designed for real-time automation. Commonly used in assembly lines and robotic systems, PLCs handle a variety of input/output operations to control machinery precisely and reliably. They are built to withstand harsh environments and operate continuously without failure.

- **Remote Terminal Units (RTUs):** RTUs are microprocessor-based devices typically deployed in remote or hard-to-reach locations. They act as communication bridges between physical equipment and central control systems, gathering field data (e.g., temperature, pressure, and flow) and transmitting it back for analysis and decision-making.

- **Human-Machine Interfaces (HMIs):** HMIs serve as the visual and interactive layer of ICS. Through graphical dashboards, alarms, and input controls, HMIs allow operators to monitor system status, respond to alerts, and adjust settings in real-time—enhancing situational awareness and operational responsiveness.

- **Supervisory Systems (e.g., SCADA):** Supervisory systems, such as **SCADA (Supervisory Control and Data Acquisition)**, provide centralized oversight of industrial operations. These platforms aggregate data from PLCs, RTUs, and HMIs to offer a high-level, real-time view of system performance, enabling centralized monitoring and control across multiple assets and locations.

In real life, the ICS environment looks like this (Figure 1-6).

CHAPTER 1 INTRODUCTION OF OPERATIONAL TECHNOLOGY (OT) SECURITY AND
INDUSTRIAL CONTROL SYSTEMS (ICS)

Figure 1-6. *ICS real-life environment example*

All ICS detailed key components will be explained in detail in Chapter 2.

OT and ICS Key Vendors

Operational Technology (OT) and Industrial Control Systems (ICS) are critical components in industrial environments, controlling physical devices and processes. The market for OT and ICS solutions involves several key vendors known for their robust offerings and technologies. Here are several prominent ones:

CHAPTER 1   INTRODUCTION OF OPERATIONAL TECHNOLOGY (OT) SECURITY AND INDUSTRIAL CONTROL SYSTEMS (ICS)

1. **Siemens**: Offers comprehensive automation solutions and is widely recognized for its SIMATIC PLCs, SCADA systems, and other industrial automation products.

2. **Schneider Electric**: Provides numerous solutions in automation and control, including their EcoStruxure platform, which is designed to support IoT and Industry 4.0 initiatives.

3. **Rockwell Automation**: Known for its Allen-Bradley line of automation products and industrial control systems, offering a range of solutions for various industries.

4. **Honeywell**: Delivers integrated automation solutions, including DCS (Distributed Control Systems), SCADA, and other cybersecurity solutions for industrial environments.

5. **ABB**: Provides offerings in process automation, electrification, robotics, and industrial automation, with strong emphasis on digital solutions and services.

6. **Emerson**: Offers process automation products and solutions, specializing in control systems, valve automation, and measurement solutions.

7. **General Electric (GE) Automation and Controls**: Provides industrial automation products and software, leveraging IoT technologies to enhance efficiency and reliability.

CHAPTER 1   INTRODUCTION OF OPERATIONAL TECHNOLOGY (OT) SECURITY AND
            INDUSTRIAL CONTROL SYSTEMS (ICS)

8. **Yokogawa**: Known for delivering comprehensive industrial automation and control solutions, particularly in the areas of production control systems.

These vendors play a pivotal role in advancing industrial operations, providing technologies that enhance efficiency, safety, and reliability. When choosing vendors, consider factors like compatibility with existing systems, technology integration capabilities, and support services.

Common Use Cases of ICS include the following:

- **Power Generation and Distribution:**

    ICS monitor turbines, substations, and transmission lines to ensure stable energy output and fault detection.

- **Water and Wastewater Management:**

    ICS regulate treatment plants, pump stations, and reservoirs to maintain water quality and supply.

- **Oil and Gas Pipelines:**

    RTUs and SCADA systems detect leaks, monitor pressure, and manage valve operations over thousands of kilometers.

- **Manufacturing and Assembly Lines:**

    PLCs automate repetitive tasks like packaging, welding, and robotic arm movement, ensuring consistency and precision.

- **Transportation Systems:**

    ICS are used in traffic light control, rail signaling, and airport baggage handling systems for safe and efficient operations.

CHAPTER 1 INTRODUCTION OF OPERATIONAL TECHNOLOGY (OT) SECURITY AND INDUSTRIAL CONTROL SYSTEMS (ICS)

Summary

In this chapter, we described the main differences between Operational Technology (OT), which refers to hardware and software systems used to monitor, control, and manage industrial processes, infrastructure, assets, etc., and Industrial Control Systems (ICS) Security, which instead refers to the protection of industrial automation and control systems used in critical infrastructure, manufacturing, and various industries.

We introduced in detail OT environments and, at general level, its key components like ICS, SCADA, etc. We defined the OT key landscapes, industries and sectors. We highlighted what IT-OT convergence means and the challenges.

Then we moved to ICS and its components, why ICs matters, and the best practices in cybersecurity.

We described in detail the key differences between ICS and OT, and finally a short introduction of the Common Use Cases of ICS.

CHAPTER 2

Key Components of Industrial Control Systems (ICS)

In the first chapter of this pocketbook, we introduced what is Operational Technology (OT), such as the hardware and software systems used to monitor, control, and manage industrial processes, infrastructure, and assets, as well as Industrial Control Systems (ICS) Security, which instead is the protection of industrial automation and control systems used in critical infrastructure, manufacturing, and various industries.

We also described why the convergence of IT and OT environments is more and more required by the digitalization era.

We introduced the increased security challenges of the ICS and OT systems, once isolated, but now more and more connected to corporate networks and the Internet, exposing them to a new array of cyber threats.

We also reminded the most typical Cybersecurity attacks on ICS/OT systems and how they can lead to catastrophic outcomes, including operational disruption, physical damages, financial losses, and threats to human safety.

CHAPTER 2 KEY COMPONENTS OF INDUSTRIAL CONTROL SYSTEMS (ICS)

In this chapter, we will focus on the ICS key components just introduced previously which include the following:

- **SCADA:** Supervisory Control And Data Acquisition system, which is a combination of hardware and software that enables the automation of industrial processes by capturing Operational Technology (OT) real-time data.

- **DCS:** Distributed Control Systems, which is a digital automated industrial control system (ICS) that uses geographically distributed control loops throughout a factory, machine, or control area.

- **PLC:** Programmable Logic Controller, which is an industrial computer control system that continuously monitors the state of input devices and makes decisions based upon a custom program to control the state of output devices.

- **RTU:** A Remote Terminal Unit is a ruggedized, microprocessor-based electronic device used in industrial and infrastructure systems to monitor and control equipment in remote or harsh environments.

- **HMI:** Human-Machine Interfaces, which is the hardware or software through which an operator interacts with a controller.

- **Controllers:** Components of ICS that maintain conformance with specifications.

- **Sensors:** Used to measure parameters such as temperature, pressure, humidity, flow rate, and other vital industrial variables.

CHAPTER 2   KEY COMPONENTS OF INDUSTRIAL CONTROL SYSTEMS (ICS)

A simplified ICS Architecture picture and its key components are shown in Figure 2-1.

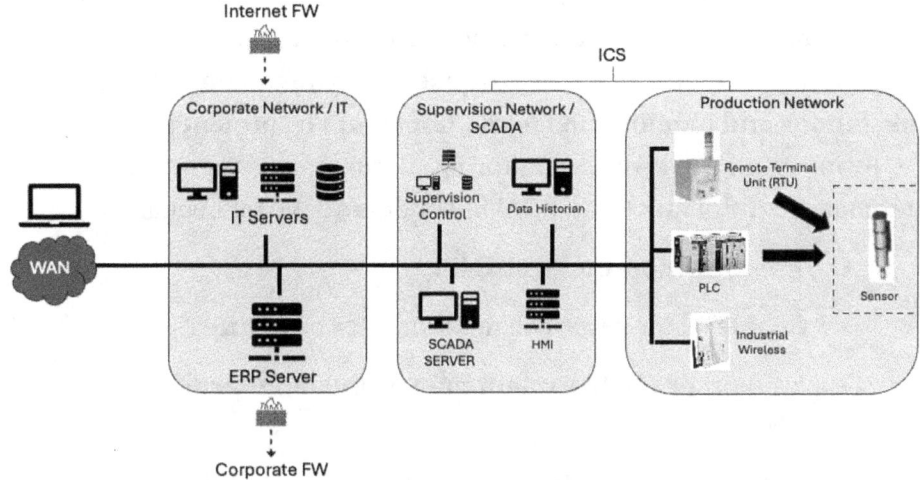

Figure 2-1. *A simplified Architecture of ICS key components*

Let's explore these ICS key components to understand better how they work in the ICS environment.

Introduction of SCADA in Its Role in Industrial Operations

SCADA (Supervisory Control and Data Acquisition) systems are a foundational element of modern **Industrial Control Systems (ICS)**, specifically designed for **high-level supervision and centralized control** of complex industrial processes. SCADA enables the **real-time collection, visualization, and analysis of data** from remote equipment and field sites, providing operators with the tools needed to manage operations efficiently across vast geographic areas.

37

CHAPTER 2 KEY COMPONENTS OF INDUSTRIAL CONTROL SYSTEMS (ICS)

In sectors such as **energy, water and wastewater management, manufacturing**, and **transportation**, operations often span multiple facilities, regions, or even countries. SCADA systems make it possible to **coordinate and control these distributed assets** from a central hub, offering a unified interface to oversee everything from **electrical substations and pipelines to factory floors and treatment plants**.

By integrating real-time monitoring, alarm management, and automated control functions, SCADA systems do the following:

- Improve **operational visibility**
- Enable **faster response to anomalies or failures**
- Support **predictive maintenance and long-term planning**
- Enhance **overall efficiency and system reliability**

Ultimately, SCADA is indispensable for managing large-scale industrial infrastructure. It not only provides the backbone for **safe and reliable operations** but also empowers organizations to make informed, data-driven decisions that optimize performance and minimize downtime.

How SCADA works?

At its heart, a SCADA system **collects real-time data, processes it, displays it for human operators**, and allows for **automated or manual control** of connected systems.

Here's how it works step by step:

1. **Data Acquisition (Sensing Layer)**

    SCADA begins by **collecting data** from sensors and field devices such as

    - Flow meters
    - Pressure sensors
    - Temperature gauges

CHAPTER 2   KEY COMPONENTS OF INDUSTRIAL CONTROL SYSTEMS (ICS)

- Switches
- Actuators

These devices are typically connected to

- **RTUs (Remote Terminal Units)**

- **PLCs (Programmable Logic Controllers)**

The sensors monitor real-time values from the physical world (e.g., water level in a reservoir) and send the information to RTUs or PLCs.

2. **Data Transmission (Communication Layer)**

The RTUs and PLCs **transmit the collected data** to the central SCADA server or control center over communication networks, which may include

- Ethernet/IP
- Serial connections (RS-232, RS-485)
- Radio, microwave, or cellular networks (especially in remote areas)
- TCP/IP over LAN/WAN

Modern SCADA systems also support secure communication protocols (e.g., DNP3 Secure, OPC UA, MQTT) to prevent cyber threats.

3. **Data Processing and Visualization (Control Layer)**

At the central SCADA server

- Data is **aggregated and stored** in databases (historian systems).

- The SCADA **software analyzes** incoming data for trends, abnormalities, or thresholds.

- Operators interact with the system using an **HMI (Human-Machine Interface)**, which displays
  - Real-time dashboards
  - Alarms and alerts
  - Historical trends
  - Control options (e.g., opening a valve, stopping a pump)

This allows operators to **monitor operations**, **respond to events**, and **make informed decisions**.

4. **Control and Automation (Action Layer)**

SCADA systems allow for both **manual and automated control** of field devices. For example:

- Automatically shutting down a pump if pressure exceeds a threshold.
- Sending a command from the control room to open/close valves remotely.
- Running scheduled automation routines.

These actions ensure **operational continuity**, **safety**, and **efficiency**—especially in environments where manual intervention may be slow or impractical.

Key Benefits of SCADA include the following:

- **Centralized Monitoring**: View the entire operation from one location.
- **Real-Time Control**: Respond instantly to system changes or failures.

- **Historical Data**: Analyze past events for maintenance or compliance.

- **Remote Accessibility**: Manage infrastructure in distant or hazardous environments.

- **Automation**: Reduce manual effort and error.

What Are the Unique Security Challenges in SCADA Systems?

SCADA systems face **distinct security challenges** due to their architecture and function:

- **Geographical Dispersion**: SCADA environments span large areas, making physical security and remote access control more difficult.

- **Legacy Infrastructure**: These systems often lack modern safeguards, having been built for reliability rather than security.

- **Proprietary Protocols**: Many SCADA systems use vendor-specific protocols that are incompatible with standard security tools, limiting the effectiveness of traditional cybersecurity measures.

Introduction of Distributed Control System (DCS)

In the realm of industrial automation and control, the **Distributed Control System (DCS)** stands out as a sophisticated and highly reliable solution for managing complex processes. DCS technology is extensively utilized across industries such as oil and gas, chemical processing, power

CHAPTER 2   KEY COMPONENTS OF INDUSTRIAL CONTROL SYSTEMS (ICS)

generation, water treatment, and pharmaceuticals. Its primary purpose is to provide precise, flexible, and secure control over manufacturing and processing operations, enhancing efficiency, safety, and productivity.

A **Distributed Control System (DCS)** is an automated control architecture that distributes control functions across multiple controllers strategically placed throughout the facility. Unlike traditional centralized control systems, a DCS decentralizes control by integrating multiple controllers connected via high-speed networks. This setup allows operators to monitor and control multiple subsystems or process areas from a centralized Human-Machine Interface (HMI) while distributing real-time control locally.

Key Components of a DCS include the following:

- **Controllers (DCS Controllers):** Embedded devices that execute control algorithms locally in process units.

- **Operator Stations (HMIs):** Interfaces for operators to monitor, control, and visualize the process.

- **Input/Output Modules (I/O):** Interface with sensors and actuators, collecting data and executing control commands.

- **Communication Network:** Robust, high-speed networks (Ethernet, IPS, etc.) connecting controllers, I/O modules, and operator stations.

- **Engineering Workstation:** For system configuration, programming, and maintenance.

- **Supervisory System:** Manages process data, archiving, alarm handling, and advanced control algorithms.

CHAPTER 2   KEY COMPONENTS OF INDUSTRIAL CONTROL SYSTEMS (ICS)

How DCS works in an ICS Environment?

A DCS operates by continuously collecting data from field devices such as temperature sensors, flow meters, and pressure transmitters. The controllers execute control loops (e.g., temperature regulation, flow control) based on this input, adjusting actuators like valves and motors to maintain process variables within desired ranges.

Data from all controllers is transmitted over the network to centralized HMIs and supervisory systems, providing operators with real-time visualization, alarms, and diagnostics. The decentralized control approach enhances system reliability because failure in one controller typically does not compromise the entire process.

Advantages of DCS in Industrial Control Systems are as follows:

1. **High Reliability and Safety:** Distributed architecture reduces single points of failure and enhances operational safety.

2. **Scalability and Flexibility:** Easily expanded by adding new controllers or modules without affecting the existing system.

3. **Improved Process Control:** Precise control loops and advanced algorithms (such as cascade, feedforward, and adaptive control) optimize process performance.

4. **Enhanced Data Management:** Centralized data collection, logging, and historian services facilitate process analysis and compliance.

5. **Operator Accessibility:** Intuitive HMIs enable operators to monitor and control processes efficiently across large facilities.

6. **Integration Capabilities:** Compatible with legacy systems and modern communication protocols for seamless integration.

Challenges of DCS are as follows:

While offering many benefits, DCS systems also face certain challenges:

- **High Initial Cost:** The sophisticated hardware and software infrastructure can be expensive.
- **Complexity:** Designing, implementing, and maintaining a DCS requires skilled personnel.
- **Cybersecurity Risks:** Increasing connectivity exposes the system to cyber threats; cybersecurity measures are essential.
- **Compatibility Issues:** Integrating with existing legacy systems or third-party equipment can be complex.

Future trends in DCS Technology

The evolution of DCS is driven by advancements in technology:

- **Integration with IoT and Industry 4.0:** Enabling real-time data analytics, predictive maintenance, and machine learning.
- **Cybersecurity Enhancements:** Incorporating advanced security protocols to counter cyber threats.
- **Hybrid Control Architectures:** Combining centralized, decentralized, and cloud-based control models.
- **Enhanced Human-Machine Interfaces:** Incorporation of AR/VR for maintenance and troubleshooting.
- **Edge Computing:** Local processing capabilities to reduce latency and bandwidth requirements.

The **Distributed Control System (DCS)** remains a cornerstone of modern industrial automation, providing scalable, reliable, and precise control over complex processes. Its distributed architecture enhances safety and operational efficiency, making it ideal for large-scale, critical industries. As technology continues to advance, DCS solutions will become more intelligent, interconnected, and secure—driving the future of industrial control in an increasingly digital world.

Differences Between DCS and ICS

The terms **Distributed Control System (DCS)** and **Industrial Control System (ICS)** are often used in automation and control environments, but they refer to different concepts with some overlapping aspects. Table 2-1 shows a clear comparison highlighting the key differences.

Table 2-1. Differences Between DCS and ICS

Aspect	Distributed Control System (DCS)	Industrial Control System (ICS)
Definition	A specialized control system designed for continuous and complex process control in large-scale industries. It distributes control functions across multiple controllers located throughout the plant.	A broad term that encompasses all automation and control systems used in industrial environments, including various control architectures like PLC, SCADA, DCS, and safety systems.
Scope	Specific type of control system primarily used in continuous, process-oriented industries such as chemical, oil and gas, power plants.	An umbrella term that covers all control systems used in industry, including DCS, PLC systems, SCADA, safety instrumented systems, etc.

(*continued*)

CHAPTER 2   KEY COMPONENTS OF INDUSTRIAL CONTROL SYSTEMS (ICS)

Table 2-1. (*continued*)

Aspect	Distributed Control System (DCS)	Industrial Control System (ICS)
Architecture	Decentralized, with control functions distributed across multiple controllers connected over high-speed networks.	Can be centralized, decentralized, or hybrid. It includes various architectures, including DCS, PLC networks, SCADA systems, etc.
Typical Application	Continuous process industries with complex control requirements (e.g., chemical plants, refineries, power generation).	Any industrial environment requiring automation and control, including discrete manufacturing, infrastructure, and distributed applications.
Control Focus	Focuses on complex, high-volume, and continuous control processes with high availability and reliability.	Includes a wide range of control applications from simple to complex, encompassing both continuous and discrete processes.
Communication Protocols	Uses specific protocols optimized for real-time process control, such as Ethernet/IP, Profibus, Foundation Fieldbus.	Uses diverse protocols depending on the system type, including Ethernet, Modbus, OPC, DNP3, etc.
Complexity & Flexibility	High complexity, designed for high reliability, scalability, and real-time control.	Varies widely—from simple control systems to highly complex networks integrating multiple control solutions.
Safety & Security	Designed with high reliability and often incorporates safety features; security is increasingly emphasized due to connectivity.	Encompasses core safety control systems as well but varies depending on the specific system components.

CHAPTER 2   KEY COMPONENTS OF INDUSTRIAL CONTROL SYSTEMS (ICS)

All DCS are a form of ICS, but not all ICS are DCS. The choice depends on the industry and process requirements, with DCS being ideal for large-scale, continuous processes.

Remember that

- **ICS** is a broad term that covers **all** control systems used in industrial automation, including **DCS**, **PLCs**, **SCADA**, and safety systems.

- **DCS** is a specific type of **control system** within the ICS landscape, optimized for continuous, complex process control in large-scale industries with a focus on distributed architecture.

Introduction of Programmable Logic Controller (PLC)

A Programmable Logic Controller (PLC) is a specialized computer used to control machines and processes in industrial environments. It is designed for real-time use and is capable of withstanding harsh conditions such as humidity, dust, and high temperatures. PLCs are integral components of Industrial Control Systems (ICS), helping automate complex processes and ensuring efficient, reliable operations.

Key Components of a PLC are as follows:

1. **Processor (CPU):** Executes control instructions based on inputs.

2. **Power Supply:** Provides necessary electrical power.

3. **Input/Output (I/O) Modules:** Interface with sensors and actuators.

CHAPTER 2   KEY COMPONENTS OF INDUSTRIAL CONTROL SYSTEMS (ICS)

4. **Communication Interfaces:** Enable data exchange with other systems.

5. **Programming Device:** Used to configure and program the PLC.

How PLCs Work?

PLCs operate by receiving input signals from various sensors (e.g., temperature, pressure, and flow sensors), processing these signals through a programmed logic sequence, and triggering corresponding outputs to control devices such as motors, valves, and alarms.

Programming Languages:

PLCs are programmed using a variety of languages, standardized under the IEC 61131-3 standard. Common languages include the following:

- **Ladder Logic:** Resembles electrical relay logic, making it intuitive for engineers with electrical backgrounds.

- **Function Block Diagram (FBD):** Describes functions in blocks, suitable for complex algorithms.

- **Structured Text:** A high-level language similar to Pascal, used for advanced programming.

- **Instruction List:** A low-level language for simple, instruction-based programs.

- **Sequential Function Chart (SFC):** Used for sequential control processes.

Applications of PLCs in ICS:

1. **Manufacturing:** Automating production lines, monitoring quality control, and managing inventory.

2. **Process Control:** Regulating processes in industries like oil and gas, chemical, and food processing.

CHAPTER 2   KEY COMPONENTS OF INDUSTRIAL CONTROL SYSTEMS (ICS)

3. **Robotics:** Controlling robotic operations and ensuring precise and safe movement.
4. **Infrastructure Management:** Used in utilities for power generation, water treatment, and building automation.

Advantages of Using PLCs:

- **Reliability:** Designed for robust and continuous operation.
- **Flexibility:** Easily reprogrammed and adaptable to different tasks.
- **Scalability:** Modular design allows for expansion as needs grow.
- **Real-Time Operation:** Process data instantaneously for timely decision-making.

Challenges and Considerations:

While PLCs offer numerous advantages, there are also challenges, including

- **Cybersecurity:** As PLCs become more networked, they are vulnerable to cyber attacks. Implementing strong cybersecurity measures is crucial.
- **Cost:** Initial setup and hardware can be expensive.
- **Complexity:** Requires skilled personnel for programming and maintenance.

Future Trends

The future of PLCs in ICS is leaning toward integration with Internet of Things (IoT) technologies, improving data analytics, and enhancing connectivity with advanced networking protocols. This evolution will pave the way for smarter, more efficient industrial operations.

PLCs are fundamental to industrial automation and control. Their ability to provide accurate, reliable, and flexible control to complex processes underscores their importance in modern industrial environments. As technology advances, PLCs will continue to evolve, offering new opportunities and challenges in optimizing industrial operations.

Introduction of Remote Terminal Units (RTUs)

Remote Terminal Units (RTUs) are vital components within the landscape of Industrial Control Systems (ICS). They serve as critical links that facilitate the collection, processing, and transmission of data between remote sites and centralized control centers. RTUs are extensively used in sectors such as energy, water treatment, oil and gas, utilities, and transportation, where large geographic areas need to be monitored and controlled efficiently.

An RTU is a rugged, specialized device designed for remote data acquisition and control in harsh environments. It gathers data from sensors and input devices at remote locations, processes this data, and transmits it to a central control system such as a Supervisory Control and Data Acquisition (SCADA) system. Conversely, RTUs also execute control commands received from the central system, enabling remote management of equipment.

Key Components of an RTU include

- **Input/Output Modules:** Interface with sensors, actuators, and other field devices for data collection and control commands.

- **Processor (Controller):** Executes control algorithms, processes data, and manages communications.

CHAPTER 2 KEY COMPONENTS OF INDUSTRIAL CONTROL SYSTEMS (ICS)

- **Communication Module:** Facilitates data exchange over various communication networks (radio, satellite, cellular, etc.).

- **Power Supply:** Ensures continuous operation, often designed with battery backup or solar power capabilities for remote deployment.

- **Enclosure:** Rugged casing protecting internal components from environmental conditions such as dust, moisture, and temperature extremes.

How RTUs work in ICS environments?

RTUs operate by continuously polling sensors and input devices to collect data such as temperature, pressure, flow rate, or switch status. This data is processed locally by the RTU's embedded logic or passed directly to the central control system across wired or wireless communications. The control system can send commands back through the RTU to manipulate equipment, such as opening a valve or starting a motor, based on pre-defined logic, alarms, or operator input.

Applications of RTUs include

1. **Power Distribution and Substations:** Monitoring voltage, current, and equipment status; controlling circuit breakers.

2. **Water and Wastewater Management:** Managing pumps, valves, and tanks remotely.

3. **Oil and Gas Pipelines:** Monitoring pipeline integrity, pressure, and flow; detecting leaks or faults.

4. **Renewable Energy:** Controlling solar or wind farm equipment, ensuring optimal operation.

5. **Transportation:** Managing signals, barriers, and station infrastructure remotely.

Advantages of RTUs are

- **Remote Operation and Monitoring:** Extend control to geographically dispersed locations.
- **Cost-Effectiveness:** Minimize the need for on-site personnel and infrastructure.
- **Reliability and Durability:** Built to withstand extreme environmental conditions.
- **Flexibility:** Compatible with multiple communication methods (radio, cellular, satellite).
- **Real-Time Data Acquisition:** Critical for timely decision-making and operational adjustments.

Challenges and security considerations are

While RTUs offer significant operational benefits, they also present challenges:

- **Cybersecurity Risks:** Remote devices increase exposure to hacking or malicious attacks. Implementing encryption, authentication, and regular updates is essential.
- **Communication Reliability:** Limited or unreliable communication links can hinder data transmission.

- **Hardware Failures:** Harsh environments can lead to hardware degradation, requiring regular maintenance or ruggedized designs.

- **Integration:** Ensuring seamless integration with existing SCADA or control systems can be complex.

Future Trends

The evolution of RTUs is moving toward more intelligent, interconnected devices that incorporate IoT (Internet of Things) capabilities. These smart RTUs can perform advanced data analytics locally, reducing latency, and improving decision support. Increased use of wireless communication and cybersecurity measures will enhance the resilience and efficiency of ICS operations.

RTUs are indispensable in the modern ICS environment, enabling remote supervision, control, and automation over vast and challenging terrains. Their robustness and flexibility contribute significantly to the efficiency, safety, and reliability of critical infrastructure systems. As technology advances, RTUs will continue to evolve, integrating smarter features and enhanced security to meet the demands of tomorrow's industrial landscape.

Human-Machine Interface (HMI)

The Human-Machine Interface (HMI) is a critical component within the framework of Industrial Control Systems (ICS). It serves as the visual and operational bridge between human operators and the control infrastructure, enabling intuitive monitoring, control, and management of industrial processes. In the complex environments of manufacturing plants, power grids, water treatment facilities, and other critical infrastructures, effective HMIs are essential to ensure safety, efficiency, and reliability.

CHAPTER 2   KEY COMPONENTS OF INDUSTRIAL CONTROL SYSTEMS (ICS)

An HMI is a user interface that allows operators to interact with machinery, systems, and processes. It can take various forms, including physical touchscreens, computer-based graphical interfaces, or a combination of both. The core purpose of an HMI is to display real-time data from the industrial process and provide control functionalities, alarms, and diagnostics in a clear, accessible manner.

Key components of an HMI are

- **Display Devices:** Touchscreens, monitors, or panels that present graphical interfaces.

- **Control Devices:** Buttons, switches, and input fields to send commands or modify setpoints.

- **HMI Software:** The application logic that provides visualization, data logging, alarm management, and control capabilities.

- **Communication Interface:** Connects the HMI to PLCs, RTUs, or other controllers to retrieve and send data.

How HMIs Function in an ICS Environment?

HMIs gather data from various sensors, controllers, and devices in the industrial process via communication protocols such as Modbus, OPC, ProfiNet, or Ethernet/IP. The software visualizes this data using graphical elements like graphs, meters, and animated diagrams, providing operators with a comprehensive understanding of system status. Additionally, operators can use HMIs to send commands to start or stop equipment, adjust parameters, acknowledge alarms, or initiate maintenance procedures.

This interaction is crucial for real-time decision-making, troubleshooting, and maintaining optimal process performance.

Applications of HMIs include

1. **Manufacturing Automation:** Monitoring production lines, machine statuses, and product quality.

2. **Power and Energy:** Visualizing grid status, substation equipment, and energy consumption.

3. **Water Treatment and Distribution:** Managing pumps, chlorination, and filtration processes.

4. **Oil and Gas:** Remote supervision of pipelines, drilling operations, and refining processes.

5. **Building Management:** Controlling HVAC, lighting, and security systems.

Advantages of using HMIs are

- **Enhanced Operator Awareness:** Real-time data visualization improves decision-making and situational awareness.

- **Simplified Control:** User-friendly interfaces reduce operator errors and facilitate quick responses.

- **Data Logging and Analysis:** Historical data can be stored for trend analysis and predictive maintenance.

- **Alarm Management:** Immediate notifications help prevent equipment failure or safety incidents.

- **Remote Access:** Modern HMIs can be accessed remotely, enabling off-site monitoring and control.

Challenges and Security considerations are as follows:
Despite benefits, HMIs also pose certain challenges:

- **Cybersecurity Threats:** HMIs connected to corporate or Internet networks are vulnerable to cyber-attacks. Security measures such as encryption, user authentication, and network segmentation are essential.

- **Design Complexity:** Poorly designed interfaces can lead to operator confusion or oversight.

- **Reliability:** Physical failures or software bugs can impact system availability.

- **Integration:** Ensuring compatibility with various controllers and legacy systems can be complex.

Future Trends

The evolution of HMIs is geared toward more advanced, intelligent, and interconnected systems:

- **Touchless and Voice Interfaces:** For enhanced safety and hygiene.

- **Augmented Reality (AR):** Overlaying operational data onto physical machinery for maintenance and troubleshooting.

- **AI Integration:** Using machine learning for predictive analytics and automatic anomaly detection.

- **Better Cybersecurity:** Developing more secure interfaces to counter rising cyber threats.

- **Mobile and Cloud-Based HMIs:** Enabling remote, anytime-anywhere access to control systems.

CHAPTER 2   KEY COMPONENTS OF INDUSTRIAL CONTROL SYSTEMS (ICS)

The Human-Machine Interface is a cornerstone of modern Industrial Control Systems, providing the vital link between operators and their industrial environments. With its ability to improve operational efficiency, safety, and decision-making, the HMI plays a pivotal role in ensuring the smooth functioning of critical infrastructure and manufacturing processes. As technology advances, HMIs will become even more sophisticated, intuitive, and secure, supporting the ongoing digital transformation of the industry worldwide.

Introduction of ICS Controllers and Sensors

In the landscape of industrial automation, **controllers** and **sensors** play pivotal roles in ensuring that industrial processes operate smoothly, safely, and efficiently. Their seamless integration forms the backbone of Industrial Control Systems (ICS), enabling real-time monitoring, regulation, and automation across diverse industries such as manufacturing, power generation, water treatment, and oil and gas. Understanding the functions, types, and interplay of controllers and sensors is essential for designing and maintaining robust industrial systems.

What Are Sensors in ICS?

Sensors are devices that measure physical or chemical parameters within an industrial environment. They convert these parameters into electrical signals that can be processed by controllers. Sensors provide the real-time data necessary for monitoring process conditions and triggering control actions.

Types of Sensors include

- **Temperature Sensors:** Thermocouples, Resistance Temperature Detectors (RTDs)
- **Pressure Sensors:** Strain gauges, piezoelectric sensors
- **Flow Sensors:** Magnetic, ultrasonic, turbine flow meters
- **Level Sensors:** Ultrasonic, radar, capacitance sensors
- **Vibration Sensors:** Accelerometers, piezoelectric sensors
- **Chemical Sensors:** pH sensors, gas detectors
- **Position Sensors:** Encoders, potentiometers

Role of sensors are

- Continuous monitoring of process variables.
- Detecting abnormalities or deviations.
- Providing data inputs for control algorithms.
- Triggering alarms and safety shutdowns.
- Ensuring process quality and safety.

What Are ICS Controllers?

Controllers refer to devices and systems responsible for regulating industrial processes based on data from sensors and the control logic embedded within controllers.

CHAPTER 2   KEY COMPONENTS OF INDUSTRIAL CONTROL SYSTEMS (ICS)

Types of controllers are

- **Manual Controllers:** Physical switches, levers operated by personnel.

- **Automated Controllers:** Programmable Logic Controllers (PLCs), Distributed Control Systems (DCS) controllers executing control algorithms.

- **Control Algorithms:** PID (Proportional-Integral-Derivative), cascade, model predictive, and adaptive control strategies.

- **Actuators:** Valves, motors, and other devices that execute control commands to adjust process variables.

Role of controllers are

- Maintaining process variables within set limits.

- Automating equipment operation, reducing operator workload.

- Enhancing safety by shutting down or isolating processes during faults.

- Optimizing efficiency and performance through advanced control strategies.

The Interplay of Sensors and Controllers in ICS

The core of any ICS is the closed-loop control process involving sensors and controllers:

1. **Data Collection:** Sensors measure parameters like temperature, pressure, or flow and transmit signals to controllers.

2. **Data Processing:** Controllers analyze the data against setpoints or control algorithms.

3. **Control Action:** Based on this analysis, controllers send commands to actuators (e.g., open a valve or start a motor).

4. **Process Adjustment:** The process responds, and sensors monitor the outcome, completing the feedback loop.

This dynamic interaction ensures processes remain stable, efficient, and within safety parameters.

Applications of Controllers and Sensors in Industry

- **Chemical and Petrochemical:** Precise temperature and pressure control for reactions.
- **Power Plants:** Monitoring turbine and boiler parameters, controlling fuel and water flow.
- **Water Treatment:** Level sensors and flow control for pumps and chemical dosing.
- **Manufacturing:** Vibration sensors for predictive maintenance, controlling robotic arms, conveyors.
- **Oil and Gas Pipelines:** Pressure sensors and flow control valves for safe transport.

Challenges in using controllers and sensors are

- **Sensor Accuracy and Calibration:** Ensuring sensors provide reliable data over time.
- **Environmental Conditions:** Sensors and controllers must withstand harsh environments like extreme temperatures, moisture, and dust.
- **System Integration:** Compatibility between sensors, controllers, and communication protocols.

CHAPTER 2   KEY COMPONENTS OF INDUSTRIAL CONTROL SYSTEMS (ICS)

- **Cybersecurity:** Protecting these systems from cyber threats, especially as they become connected.

- **Reliability and Maintenance:** Ensuring continuous operation and quick maintenance response.

Future Trends in Controllers and Sensors

- **Smart Sensors:** Integration with IoT for predictive maintenance and remote diagnostics.

- **Wireless Sensors:** Flexible deployment without extensive wiring.

- **Advanced Control Algorithms:** Use of AI and machine learning for adaptive control.

- **Enhanced Cybersecurity:** Secure protocols and encryption.

- **Digital Twins:** Virtual models for simulation, testing, and optimization.

Controllers and sensors are fundamental to the operation of modern ICS environments. Sensors provide the vital data that controllers use to make real-time decisions, enabling automation, safety, and efficiency. Their continuous evolution, driven by advancements in IoT, AI, and cybersecurity, promises smarter, more resilient, and highly adaptable industrial systems in the future.

Figure 2-2 shows how HMI, SCADA, PLC, RTU, and Sensors are connected.

CHAPTER 2 KEY COMPONENTS OF INDUSTRIAL CONTROL SYSTEMS (ICS)

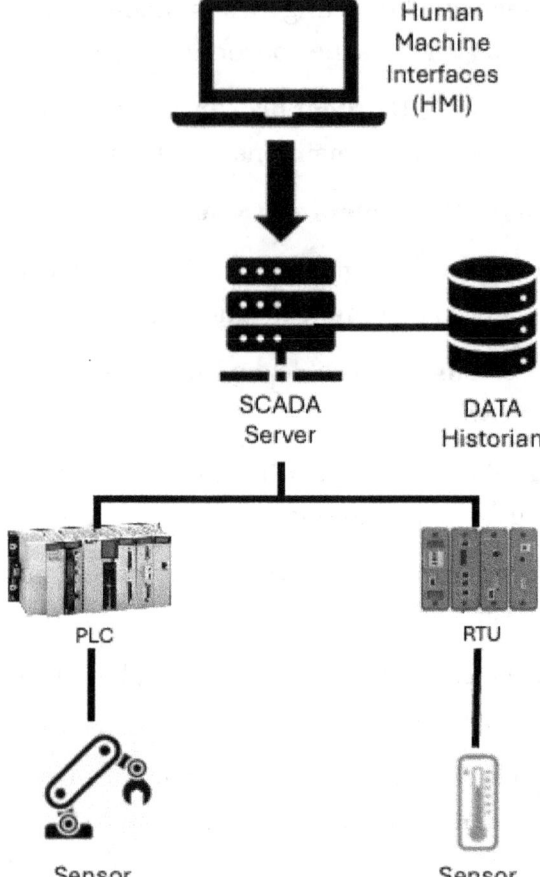

Figure 2-2. ICS key elements connections

Summary

In this chapter, we focused on the ICS key components just introduced previously, which included the Supervisory Control And Data Acquisition (**SCADA**) system—which is a combination of hardware and software that enables the automation of industrial processes by capturing Operational Technology (**OT**) real-time data; the Programmable Logic Controller (**PLC**)—which is an industrial computer control system that continuously

CHAPTER 2   KEY COMPONENTS OF INDUSTRIAL CONTROL SYSTEMS (ICS)

monitors the state of input devices and makes decisions based upon a custom program to control the state of output device; Remote Terminal Unit (**RTU**)—which is a ruggedized, microprocessor-based electronic device used in industrial and infrastructure systems to monitor and control equipment in remote or harsh environments; and Human Machine Interfaces (**HMI**)—which are the hardware or software through which an operator interacts with the **Controllers**, which are components of ICS that maintain conformance with specifications and sensors.

We introduced all these ICS key elements and how they are connected to each other.

CHAPTER 3

Challenges and Cybersecurity Attacks in Operational Technology (OT) and Industrial Control Systems (ICS)

In today's interconnected world, Industrial Control Systems (ICS) are vital to the functioning of critical infrastructure sectors such as energy, water, transportation, and manufacturing. These systems ensure the seamless operation of complex industrial processes by monitoring, controlling, and automating essential functions.

However, as industries embrace digital transformation and increased connectivity, ICS environments are exposed to a growing array of vulnerabilities and challenges. Traditional ICS, once isolated and secure, are now more integrated with corporate IT networks and the Internet, increasing their exposure to cyber threats.

CHAPTER 3   CHALLENGES AND CYBERSECURITY ATTACKS IN OPERATIONAL
             TECHNOLOGY (OT) AND INDUSTRIAL CONTROL SYSTEMS (ICS)

At the same time, many ICS components are based on legacy technologies that lack modern security features. This creates a landscape where potential security breaches could have severe consequences, ranging from operational disruptions to safety hazards and economic losses.

Operational Technology (OT) environments, such as factories, power plants, and critical infrastructure, are increasingly becoming digital and interconnected. While these advancements improve efficiency and automation, they also introduce new cybersecurity risks. Protecting OT systems is complex due to their unique characteristics and operational requirements.

Moreover, the complexity of managing and maintaining these systems presents additional challenges. Balancing the requirements of reliability, safety, and efficiency while implementing robust security measures is a delicate task.

This chapter dives into the vulnerabilities that make ICS susceptible to attacks and the multifaceted challenges organizations face in safeguarding these crucial systems—highlighting the urgent need for comprehensive security strategies tailored to the unique demands of ICS environments.

Also, we will discuss the evolution of ICS and OT security and how the cybersecurity attacks started to involve also that environment.

The Growing Cyber Threat to Industrial Operations

In today's hyper-connected world, industrial control systems (ICS) and operational technology (OT) are under constant cyber threat. Ransomware, insider threats, and nation-state attacks are targeting manufacturing plants, energy grids, smart buildings, and critical infrastructure—leading to devastating downtime, compliance violations, and financial losses.

CHAPTER 3 CHALLENGES AND CYBERSECURITY ATTACKS IN OPERATIONAL TECHNOLOGY (OT) AND INDUSTRIAL CONTROL SYSTEMS (ICS)

The major reasons why Industrial Cybersecurity is critical include the following:

- Rising Cyber Threats in Industrial Environments.
- IT–OT Convergence Risks.
- Lack of OT Network Visibility and Monitoring.
- Compliance and Regulatory Requirements.
- Industrial Downtime Is Costly.
- Risk Management.
- Integration with Existing Systems.
- Incident Response.
- Tailored Solutions.

Let's have a look at the history of the evolution of ICS and OT Cybersecurity.

Industrial Control Systems (ICS) and Operational Technology (OT) have undergone a remarkable transformation from isolated, proprietary systems to highly interconnected and digitized environments. Originally designed for reliability and performance, ICS networks lacked robust cybersecurity measures due to their separation from external networks. However, with the advent of IT/OT convergence, remote access, and the rise of sophisticated cyber threats, protecting these systems has become a critical priority.

Let's take a closer look at the history and milestones that have shaped the evolution of ICS and OT cybersecurity—highlighting key technological shifts, major incidents, and emerging defense strategies.

CHAPTER 3 CHALLENGES AND CYBERSECURITY ATTACKS IN OPERATIONAL TECHNOLOGY (OT) AND INDUSTRIAL CONTROL SYSTEMS (ICS)

Here are some of the most important steps of the evolution of ICS and OT Security:

1. **Early ICS Era (Pre-2000s): Isolated and Proprietary**

   In the early days, ICS environments were largely isolated from external networks and used proprietary communication protocols. Security was minimal or non-existent, based on the assumption that "air-gapped" systems were safe.

   - **Characteristics:**
     - Limited connectivity
     - Security by obscurity
     - Proprietary protocols (e.g., Modbus, DNP3)
     - Focus on availability and reliability over security

2. **Integration Phase (2000s–2010s): IT/OT Convergence Begins**

   The introduction of Ethernet, TCP/IP, and Windows-based HMIs (Human-Machine Interfaces) into ICS networks marked a significant turning point. Connectivity improved efficiency and control but opened ICS to traditional IT vulnerabilities.

   - **Changes:**
     - Remote access introduced for monitoring and maintenance
     - Adoption of IT-based platforms and OS
     - Increased exposure to malware and targeted attacks (e.g., Stuxnet in 2010)

3. **Modern Era (2010s–2020s): Cybersecurity Becomes Critical**

    The rising number of cyberattacks targeting critical infrastructure forced industries to re-evaluate their security posture. ICS and OT security became a board-level concern, leading to the development of standards and frameworks.

    - **Key Developments:**

        - Emergence of standards: ISA/IEC 62443, NIST SP 800-82

        - Network segmentation, firewalls, and intrusion detection systems (IDS)

        - Growing awareness of supply chain risks

        - Adoption of Security Information and Event Management (SIEM) tools in OT

Why Is the ICS Environment Considered Challenging?

Industrial Control Systems (ICS) operate in a uniquely complex and demanding environment, which presents numerous challenges for security, maintenance, and operational stability. Several factors contribute to the difficulty of managing and safeguarding ICS:

- **Legacy Systems and Obsolete Technology:** Many ICS components were deployed decades ago and were designed with little regard for cybersecurity. These legacy systems often lack modern security features, making them vulnerable to cyber threats. Upgrading or replacing these systems is costly and technically complex, especially when they are critical to ongoing operations.

- **High Availability and Reliability Requirements:** Industrial processes demand continuous operation—downtime can lead to significant safety risks, financial losses, or environmental damage. This necessity for high availability limits the ability to conduct regular maintenance or patch systems, creating a complex balance between security and operational continuity.

- **Operational and Safety Priorities:** Safety is paramount in ICS environments. Any security measures introduced must not compromise the safety and stability of operations. Implementing security controls that interfere with real-time control or safety functions can be risky, making it challenging to adopt aggressive cybersecurity measures.

- **Heterogeneity and Complexity:** ICS environments comprise a diverse set of devices, protocols, and systems from multiple vendors, often with incompatible architectures. Managing and securing this heterogeneous landscape requires specialized knowledge and tailored solutions, complicating security management.

- **Limited Security Awareness and Resources:** Many organizations operating ICS lack dedicated cybersecurity expertise, especially in operational technology domains. Often, there's insufficient investment in security measures, training, and resources, leaving systems more exposed.

- **Connectivity and Increased Attack Surface:** The integration of ICS with corporate IT networks, remote access capabilities, and IoT devices broadens the attack surface. Cybercriminals and nation-state actors exploit these connections to launch targeted attacks, including malware, ransomware, and sabotage.

- **Physical and Environmental Constraints:** ICS components are often located in harsh environments—such as oil rigs, chemical plants, or remote substations—making physical security and maintenance challenging. Harsh conditions can also accelerate hardware degradation, complicating operational stability.

- **Difficulty in Detecting and Responding to Threats:** Traditional IT security tools are not always effective in ICS because of real-time requirements and proprietary protocols. Detecting malicious activity without disrupting ongoing operations requires specialized security solutions, which are not always available or implemented.

The combination of technological, operational, safety, and environmental factors makes ICS a particularly challenging environment to secure and manage. Successfully safeguarding these critical systems requires a deep understanding of industrial processes, specialized security measures, and strategic planning to address their unique complexities and vulnerabilities.

CHAPTER 3   CHALLENGES AND CYBERSECURITY ATTACKS IN OPERATIONAL TECHNOLOGY (OT) AND INDUSTRIAL CONTROL SYSTEMS (ICS)

OT Security Problems to Be Solved

Let's introduce now some of the most important OT Security problems to be solved.

Security complexities within OT environments are unique mainly for the following reasons:

- **Each environment is built for purpose and is unique.**
- **Multiple technologies and protocols built for and over decades.**
- **Systems designed without cybersecurity concerns.**
- **Criticality of systems means non-intrusive and very low footprint solutions need to be deployed.**

Operational Technology (OT) security faces several distinctive challenges that need to be addressed to ensure robust protection of industrial and critical infrastructure environments. Here are some typical OT security problems:

1. **Inadequate or weak Security of Remote Access Management: Authentication and Authorization:** Weak or poorly managed remote access—particularly in terms of authentication and authorization—can lead to unauthorized users gaining access to critical industrial systems. This creates opportunities for cyberattacks, such as malware infiltration, data theft, or sabotage. Strong authentication methods (like multi-factor authentication) and strict access controls are vital to ensure that only authorized personnel can access sensitive OT systems, protecting against potential threats and maintaining operational safety.

2. **Legacy Systems Vulnerabilities:** Many OT environments still use legacy systems and equipment that were not designed with modern cybersecurity standards in mind. These systems may lack built-in security features or updates, making them vulnerable to exploitation.

3. **Lack of Network Segmentation:** OT networks often lack proper segmentation from IT networks. This absence can lead to increased risk of cyber threats spreading across the entire infrastructure if one part is compromised.

4. **Insufficient Patch Management:** Regular patching of OT devices and systems is often neglected due to concerns over operational downtime or compatibility issues with critical processes. This leaves systems vulnerable to known exploits.

5. **Inadequate Authentication and Authorization:** Weak authentication mechanisms, such as default passwords or shared credentials, are common in OT environments. Additionally, insufficient authorization controls may allow unauthorized access to critical systems.

6. **Limited Visibility and Monitoring:** Many OT systems lack comprehensive monitoring capabilities, making it challenging to detect unusual activities or potential security breaches in real time.

7. **Physical Security Risks:** Physical access to OT components is often not adequately controlled, which can lead to unauthorized tampering or theft of sensitive equipment and data.

8. **Human Factors and Training:** Employees and contractors may not receive sufficient training on cybersecurity best practices specific to OT environments. This lack of awareness can result in unintentional security incidents.

9. **Integration with IT Security Policies:** OT and IT departments may operate with different security policies and practices, leading to inconsistencies and gaps in overall security posture.

10. **Supply Chain Vulnerabilities:** OT environments rely on a complex supply chain for equipment and services, which can introduce security risks if vendors do not adhere to robust cybersecurity standards.

11. **Emerging Threat Landscape:** OT systems are increasingly targeted by sophisticated cyber threats, including ransomware, advanced persistent threats (APTs), and targeted attacks aimed at disrupting critical infrastructure operations.

12. **Roles Challenges:** CISO, CIO, OT Director, etc.; when converging IT and OT, of course, it is very complicated to define IT and OT new roles and responsibilities.

Addressing these challenges requires a holistic approach that combines technical solutions, policy frameworks, and ongoing awareness and training initiatives tailored to the unique requirements of OT environments.

CHAPTER 3   CHALLENGES AND CYBERSECURITY ATTACKS IN OPERATIONAL
            TECHNOLOGY (OT) AND INDUSTRIAL CONTROL SYSTEMS (ICS)

The major OT/ICS concerns include, in general, the following:

- **Risks and impacts are high.**
- **Safety, availability, reliability, and predictability.**
- **OT/IoT/IIoT security skills are limited.**
- **Data protection and regulatory compliance.**

Let's elaborate them.

Risks and Impacts are high:

- **Details:** In industrial environments, failures or breaches can cause physical damage to equipment, environmental harm, or threaten human safety. For example:

  - A cyberattack on a nuclear power plant's control system could potentially lead to dangerous radioactive leaks.

  - Compromised water treatment systems might lead to unsafe water being supplied to the public.

- **Impact:** The repercussions can be catastrophic, including loss of life, environmental disasters, costly downtime, and loss of public trust. Therefore, these risks demand stringent security measures, continuous monitoring, and rapid response plans.

- **Strategies:**

  - **Conduct Regular Risk Assessments:** Identify vulnerabilities and potential impact scenarios. Use tools like FMEA (Failure Mode and Effects Analysis) and threat modeling.

- **Implement Defense-in-Depth:** Use layered security controls, including firewalls, intrusion detection systems, segmentation, and access controls.

- **Develop Incident Response and Business Continuity Plans:** Prepare protocols for rapid containment, mitigation, and recovery.

- **Invest in Physical Security:** Control physical access to critical systems and devices.

- **Best Practices:**

  - Collaborate with cybersecurity experts specialized in ICS environments.

  - Continuously update and patch systems, where possible, to mitigate known vulnerabilities.

  - Monitor systems 24/7 for suspicious activity using SIEM (Security Information and Event Management) solutions.

Safety, availability, reliability, and predictability:

- **Details:**

  - **Safety:** Systems must prevent accidents, such as machinery overpressure or toxic leaks, that could endanger workers or the public.

  - **Availability:** Power grids or manufacturing lines need to operate 24/7; disruptions can cost millions per hour.

  - **Reliability:** Systems should perform correctly over long periods without unexpected failures.

- **Predictability:** Maintenance schedules depend on understanding system behavior; unexpected variabilities can cause failures.

- **Examples:**

  - Emergency shutdown systems in a chemical plant must trigger reliably without failure.

  - Power grids use predictive analytics to anticipate demand peaks and avoid outages.

- **Strategies:**

  - **Implement Redundancy:** Use multiple controllers, power supplies, and communication paths to ensure continuous operation.

  - **Regular Maintenance and Testing:** Use predictive analytics and condition-based monitoring to schedule maintenance proactively.

  - **Certified Safety Protocols:** Follow industry standards like IEC 62443 and ISA/IEC 61511 for safety instrumented systems.

  - **Use Real-Time Monitoring:** Deploy sensors and analytics to constantly assess system status and predict failures.

- **Best Practices:**

  - Maintain detailed logs for troubleshooting and compliance.

  - Train staff on safety procedures and emergency protocols.

  - Use simulation and modeling to predict system responses under different conditions.

CHAPTER 3 CHALLENGES AND CYBERSECURITY ATTACKS IN OPERATIONAL TECHNOLOGY (OT) AND INDUSTRIAL CONTROL SYSTEMS (ICS)

OT/IoT/IIoT Security skills are limited:

- **Details:** Many organizations lack personnel who fully understand both operational processes and cybersecurity. As these systems are often legacy or specialized, cybersecurity best practices are not always well-understood or implemented.

    - **Examples:**
        - An IoT-enabled water sensor lacks proper security protocols, making it vulnerable to hacking, which could cause false alarms or tampering.
        - Legacy PLC (Programmable Logic Controller) systems may not support modern security features, increasing vulnerability.

    - **Implication:** Without specialized skills, organizations risk delayed threat detection or ineffective responses, which can escalate an attack.

Data protection and regulatory compliance:

- **Details:** Data collected in ICS—such as operational metrics, control commands, or environmental data—must be protected from unauthorized access or alteration.

- **Examples:**
    - Failing to comply with regulations like NERC CIP in the energy sector can result in hefty fines.
    - Personal data involved in certain operations, like employee information, must be safeguarded under GDPR.

- **Implication:** Non-compliance can lead to legal penalties, and data breaches can further threaten operational integrity and safety.

- **Strategies:**

  - **Implement Encryption:** Use encryption for data at rest and in transit.

  - **Access Controls:** Enforce strict user authentication, role-based access, and audit logs.

  - **Regular Audits and Compliance Checks:** Conduct internal and external audits to ensure adherence to relevant standards.

  - **Develop Data Handling Policies:** Define clear procedures for data collection, storage, and disposal.

- **Best Practices:**

  - Use automated compliance tools to track adherence.

  - Keep detailed records of security measures and incidents for audit purposes.

  - Regularly update policies based on changing regulations and technological developments.

Introduction of Cybersecurity Attack in OT/ICS Environment

As industrial control systems (ICS) become increasingly interconnected with corporate networks, cloud services, and the wider Internet, their exposure to cybersecurity threats has grown exponentially. Historically

CHAPTER 3   CHALLENGES AND CYBERSECURITY ATTACKS IN OPERATIONAL
             TECHNOLOGY (OT) AND INDUSTRIAL CONTROL SYSTEMS (ICS)

isolated and designed without security considerations, many ICS environments now face a rising tide of sophisticated cyber-attacks aimed at disrupting critical infrastructure, causing operational failures, or extracting sensitive data.

Cybercriminals, nation-states, and hacktivist groups are targeting ICS due to their strategic importance and potential for widespread impact. Attacks against these systems can lead to severe consequences, including safety hazards, environmental disasters, significant financial losses, and compromised national security.

Understanding the nature of cybersecurity threats faced by ICS environments is essential for developing effective defense strategies, ensuring operational continuity, and safeguarding critical infrastructure from malicious actors.

A Brief History of Cybersecurity Attacks on ICS

The evolution of cybersecurity threats targeting industrial control systems (ICS) reflects the broader development of digital technology and cyber warfare. Historically, ICS environments were isolated, making them less vulnerable to cyber threats. However, as connectivity increased, so did the risk landscape.

Early incidents and recognized threats reported are as follows:

- **1970s–1980s:** The initial recognition of cybersecurity vulnerabilities in industrial environments was limited, as most ICS were isolated, proprietary, and not connected to external networks.

- **2000s:** With the advent of IP-based protocols and increased networking in industrial environments, vulnerabilities grew. Cybercriminals began exploiting these weaknesses, though attacks remained relatively infrequent and less sophisticated.

CHAPTER 3 CHALLENGES AND CYBERSECURITY ATTACKS IN OPERATIONAL TECHNOLOGY (OT) AND INDUSTRIAL CONTROL SYSTEMS (ICS)

Notable milestones and incidents reported are as follows:

- **Stuxnet (2010):** Arguably the most infamous ICS-related cyberattack, Stuxnet was a sophisticated computer worm believed to be developed by nation-states. It targeted Iran's nuclear program by sabotaging uranium enrichment centrifuges. Stuxnet demonstrated that cyber weapons could cause physical damage to industrial equipment—a game-changing moment in cybersecurity for ICS.

- **Industroyer/CrashOverride (2016–2017):** These malware strains targeted electrical grids and power infrastructure in Europe, showing that nation-states and organized hacking groups can manipulate power systems through cyber means.

- **Triton/Trisis (2017):** A zero-day attack targeted safety instrumented systems (SIS) in a petrochemical plant, aiming to cause operational disruptions or endanger lives—highlighting the dangerous potential of cyberattacks on safety-critical systems.

Cybersecurity Threats and Incidents in ICS in 2022–2025

Let's have a look at the Cybersecurity threats and incidents in ICS/OT during the period of 2022–2025.

In 2022:

- **Increasing Ransomware Attacks on Critical Infrastructure:**

CHAPTER 3 CHALLENGES AND CYBERSECURITY ATTACKS IN OPERATIONAL TECHNOLOGY (OT) AND INDUSTRIAL CONTROL SYSTEMS (ICS)

Throughout 2022, ransomware targeting ICS and industrial networks became more frequent, with threat actors focusing on disrupting operations of energy providers, manufacturing facilities, and transportation systems. These attacks often leveraged known vulnerabilities or used phishing to gain initial access, emphasizing the importance of robust cybersecurity protocols.

- **Notable Attack on Power Grids:**

    Several incidents involved coordinated attacks on electrical grid operators, highlighting the ongoing threat posed by nation-states and organized hacking groups seeking to destabilize critical infrastructure.

- **Supply Chain Vulnerabilities:**

    The year also saw increased attention on supply chain security, as compromised hardware and software components introduced vulnerabilities into ICS environments. Attacks like those exploiting vulnerabilities in third-party vendors underscored the need for comprehensive supply chain risk management.

In 2023:

- **Emergence of Autonomous and AI-Driven Attacks:**

    Advances in AI and machine learning enabled attackers to develop more sophisticated, automated attack vectors against ICS. These included adaptive malware capable of bypassing traditional security measures and executing stealthy, targeted operations.

- **Targeted Attacks on Water and Waste Management:**

    Cyber actors targeted water treatment facilities and wastewater management systems, risking contamination, service disruptions, and environmental harm. The attacks demonstrated that even previously lower-profile sectors were now within the threat landscape.

- **Government and Industry Response:**

    Governments worldwide increased investments in ICS cybersecurity, issuing stricter guidelines and establishing specialized incident response teams. Initiatives like the US Cybersecurity Workforce Development and the European Union's NIS2 directive aimed to bolster defenses.

In 2024:

- **Major Disruption in Manufacturing Sector:**

    A coordinated ransomware attack in late 2024 caused major shutdowns at several automotive manufacturing plants across Europe and North America. The attackers exploited unpatched vulnerabilities, emphasizing the importance of patch management and real-time monitoring.

- **Zero-Day Exploits and Supply Chain Attacks:**

    Hackers exploited zero-day vulnerabilities in industrial control devices and firmware updates, leading to widespread concern over the security of IoT-enabled ICS components. Supply chain infiltrations became a prominent attack vector, prompting tighter security controls and audits.

- **Enhanced Security Measures:**

  Organizations adopted more advanced defense strategies, such as AI-based anomaly detection, zero-trust architectures, and increased network segmentation, aiming to reduce the impact of potential breaches.

In 2025:

- **Escalation of State-Sponsored Operations:**

  Indicators suggest that state-backed actors are intensifying operations targeting energy, transportation, and manufacturing sectors, with an increasing focus on disrupting critical supply chains and logistics.

- **Implementation of Post-Quantum Security:**

  Research into quantum-resistant cryptographic protocols gained momentum, as the threat of quantum computing breaking traditional encryption could jeopardize ICS security in the future.

- **Focus on Resilience and Recovery:**

  The emphasis shifted from purely preventive measures to building system resilience, with organizations investing in rapid incident response plans, backup systems, and cyber-physical safety protocols.

- **Increased Regulatory Frameworks:**

  Governments worldwide began deploying stricter cybersecurity regulations, including mandatory reporting of incidents, regular audits, and certification standards for ICS environments.

CHAPTER 3   CHALLENGES AND CYBERSECURITY ATTACKS IN OPERATIONAL TECHNOLOGY (OT) AND INDUSTRIAL CONTROL SYSTEMS (ICS)

From 2022 to 2025, ICS cybersecurity landscape has evolved from sporadic targeted attacks to sophisticated, multi-vector operations driven by nation-states, cybercriminals, and disruptive hacktivists. As threats grow in complexity and scale, industries and governments are investing heavily in advanced security measures, resilience strategies, and international cooperation to protect critical infrastructure. Vigilance, continuous improvement, and a proactive cybersecurity posture remain essential in safeguarding the vital systems upon which modern society depends.

Top ICS/OT Cybersecurity Threats in 2025

In recent years, several factors have contributed to the rise in ICS cybersecurity incidents:

- Greater integration of ICS with corporate networks, increasing attack surface.
- Rise of ransomware targeting critical infrastructure.
- Nation-state cyber warfare capabilities expanding globally.
- Growing awareness and disclosure of vulnerabilities, encouraging more research and threat activity.

In 2025, ICS environments will face increasingly complex and targeted cyber threats, emphasizing the need for proactive security strategies, advanced threat detection, and resilient architecture to safeguard critical infrastructure.

CHAPTER 3 CHALLENGES AND CYBERSECURITY ATTACKS IN OPERATIONAL TECHNOLOGY (OT) AND INDUSTRIAL CONTROL SYSTEMS (ICS)

Here are listed the most relevant OT/ICS cybersecurity threats reported in 2025:

1. **Ransomware Targeting Critical Infrastructure:**

   a. **Description:** Increased ransomware attacks aimed at ICS environments, disrupting operations in sectors like energy, manufacturing, and water treatment.

   b. **Impact:** Extended downtime, safety risks, substantial financial losses, and compromised safety systems.

2. **Supply Chain Attacks:**

   a. **Description:** Attackers compromising ICS components during manufacturing or updates, leading to widespread vulnerabilities once deployed.

   b. **Impact:** Chain reactions across multiple sectors, difficult detection, and long-term compromised assets.

3. **IoT/IIoT Exploits:**

   a. **Description:** Cybercriminals exploiting poorly secured IoT devices integrated into industrial networks to gain footholds.

   b. **Impact:** Access to sensitive operations, lateral movement, and potential sabotage or theft.

4. **Advanced Persistent Threats (APTs):**

   a. **Description:** State-sponsored or highly organized groups conducting long-term espionage, sabotage, or data exfiltration.

   b. **Impact:** Espionage, disruption of critical services, or even active sabotage of physical assets.

5. **Legacy Systems and Zero-Day Vulnerabilities:**

    a. **Description:** Exploitation of outdated or unsupported ICS hardware and software with known or unknown vulnerabilities.

    b. **Impact:** Quick, widespread attacks leveraging unpatched vulnerabilities, leading to system shutdowns or sabotage.

6. **Artificial Intelligence (AI)-Driven Attacks:**

    a. **Description:** Use of AI to craft smarter phishing, malware, or intrusion techniques tailored to ICS environments.

    b. **Impact:** More sophisticated, adaptive attacks that bypass traditional security measures.

7. **Remote Work and Cloud Adoption Risks:**

    a. **Description:** Increased attack surface due to remote access, cloud-based management, and third-party vendors.

    b. **Impact:** Higher risk of breaches due to misconfigurations, weak controls, or insider threats.

Figure 3-1 shows the IBM X-Force Threat Intelligence Index 2024 about which OT industries were the most attacked in 2024.

CHAPTER 3   CHALLENGES AND CYBERSECURITY ATTACKS IN OPERATIONAL TECHNOLOGY (OT) AND INDUSTRIAL CONTROL SYSTEMS (ICS)

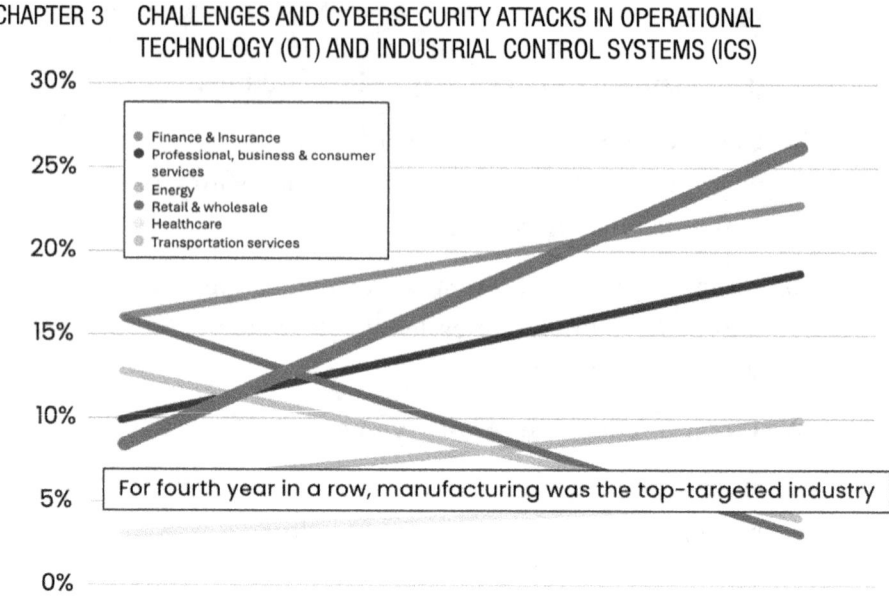

Figure 3-1. *Source: IBM X-Force Threat Intelligence Index 2024*

The major motivations of OT/ICS attacks are shown in Figure 3-2.

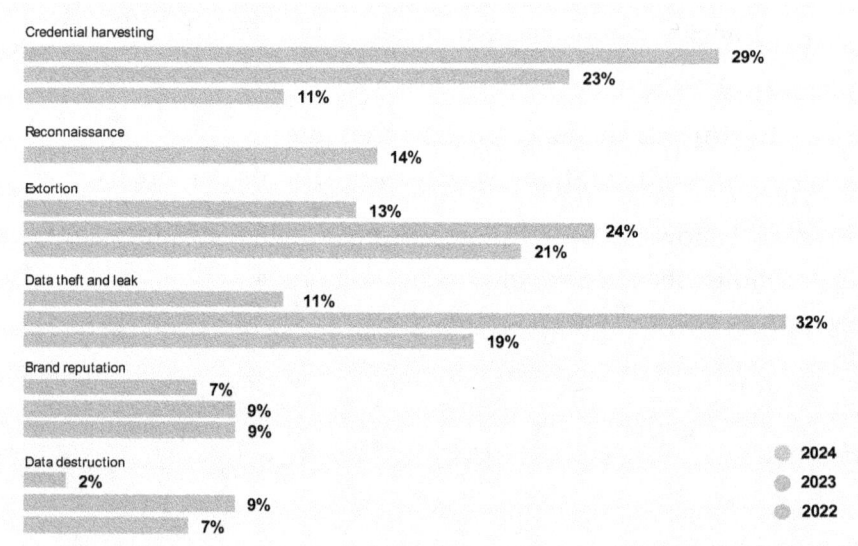

Figure 3-2. *Motivations of OT/ICS attacks in 2024*

CHAPTER 3 CHALLENGES AND CYBERSECURITY ATTACKS IN OPERATIONAL TECHNOLOGY (OT) AND INDUSTRIAL CONTROL SYSTEMS (ICS)

Emerging Technologies in ICS and OT Cybersecurity

Here are listed the emerging technologies in ICS and OT Security:

1. **Artificial Intelligence (AI) and Machine Learning (ML):**

    - **Role:** Automate anomaly detection, threat prediction, and decision-making.

    - **Benefits:** Reduce false positives, enable real-time analysis, and adapt to evolving threats.

    - **Example:** AI-driven sensors monitor system behaviors and alert operators to subtle deviations indicating cyber intrusion or physical faults.

2. **Security Orchestration, Automation, and Response (SOAR):**

    - **Role:** Automate incident response workflows specific to OT systems.

    - **Benefits:** Minimize human intervention, accelerate threat mitigation, and reduce operational impact.

    - **Use case:** Automated quarantine of compromised devices and notification workflows during attack detection.

3. **Advanced Endpoint Detection for OT Devices:**

    - **Role:** Secure IoT and IIoT devices with embedded security solutions.

    - **Benefits:** Detect malicious activity directly on devices with limited security capabilities, preventing lateral movement.

4. **Blockchain for Data Integrity and Supply Chain Security:**

    - **Role:** Use blockchain to verify authenticity, integrity, and transparency of software updates, hardware components, and sensor data.

    - **Benefits:** Deter tampering, ensure provenance, and strengthen trust in supply chain processes.

5. **Edge Computing and 5G Connectivity:**

    - **Role:** Enable real-time data processing at the network edge with high speed and low latency.

    - **Benefits:** Immediate threat detection and response locally, reducing reliance on central systems and bandwidth.

Strategic frameworks and best practices include the following:

1. **Risk-Based Security Approach:**

    - Focus on identifying critical assets and potential impact, prioritizing security investments based on risk levels.

2. **Defense-in-Depth:**

    - Employ multi-layered security measures, including network segmentation, access controls, encryptions, and real-time monitoring.

3. **Security by Design:**

    - Incorporate security features during system design and procurement, not as an afterthought.

4. **Continuous Monitoring and Incident Response:**

    - Establish ongoing system health checks and real-time detection mechanisms to manage emerging threats proactively.

5. **Supply Chain Security and Vendor Management:**

    - Enforce strict vendor vetting, secure firmware/software validation, and audit supply chain partners regularly.

6. **Regulatory Compliance and Standards:**

    - Stay aligned with evolving standards like IEC 62443, NISTIR 8228, and industry-specific regulations to ensure legal adherence and security robustness.

Key recommendations for Strategy implementation for ICS/OT Security include the following:

- **Invest in cybersecurity talent** specialized in OT environments.

- **Develop a resilience plan** that prioritizes quick recovery and system robustness.

- **Pilot new technologies** incrementally, ensuring they integrate smoothly with existing systems.

- **Foster cross-disciplinary collaboration** between IT, OT, security, and management teams.

CHAPTER 3   CHALLENGES AND CYBERSECURITY ATTACKS IN OPERATIONAL
TECHNOLOGY (OT) AND INDUSTRIAL CONTROL SYSTEMS (ICS)

Future of OT and ICS Cybersecurity

The evolution of ICS and OT security mirrors the broader digital transformation of industry. From isolated systems with minimal defenses to interconnected networks under constant threat, the shift has been profound. Looking forward, security must be proactive, adaptive, and built into every layer of ICS infrastructure.

Organizations that embrace a forward-looking, holistic approach—integrating advanced technology, regulatory compliance, and human expertise—will be best positioned to defend their operations and maintain resilience in the face of growing cyber threats.

The future of ICS and OT cybersecurity lies in proactive, intelligent, and automated security strategies—integrating advanced technologies with rigorous management practices. Emphasis will also grow on resilience, supply chain security, and regulatory compliance, crafting a more secure landscape for critical infrastructure.

As we move further into the 2020s and beyond, the future of ICS and OT security will be shaped by several trends and innovations:

1. **Zero Trust Architecture (ZTA) for OT**

    Zero Trust principles—"never trust, always verify"—will be increasingly adopted in OT environments. Every device, user, and data flow must be authenticated and authorized.

    - Micro-segmentation of networks
    - Identity-based access control
    - Continuous monitoring and behavior analytics

2. **Integration of Artificial Intelligence (AI) and Machine Learning (ML)**

   AI/ML will enhance anomaly detection, predictive maintenance, and threat intelligence by analyzing vast volumes of OT data in real time.

   - Detecting subtle anomalies in SCADA/PLC behavior
   - Predicting failures or cyberattacks before they occur
   - Automating incident response in critical environments

3. **Cloud and Edge Computing in ICS**

   The adoption of cloud and edge technologies will bring scalability and real-time analytics to ICS. However, this also expands the attack surface.

   - **Edge** computing reduces latency and allows localized data processing.
   - **Cloud** platforms enable centralized visibility and analytics.
   - It requires advanced encryption, access control, and data integrity assurance.

4. **Secure-by-Design Systems**

   Manufacturers will increasingly design ICS and OT devices with embedded security features from the outset, rather than adding security as an afterthought.

- Secure boot, encrypted communications, hardware-based trust anchors
- Adherence to secure development lifecycle (SDL) practices

5. **Regulatory and Compliance Pressure**

   Governments and international bodies are imposing stricter regulations on critical infrastructure security. Compliance will drive improved practices and increased investment in OT cybersecurity.

   - EU's NIS2 Directive
   - US Executive Orders on Critical Infrastructure
   - Sector-specific regulations (e.g., energy, transportation, and water)

6. **Cyber-Physical System Resilience**

   Future strategies will focus on resilience, not just protection—assuming breaches may occur and preparing systems to recover safely and quickly.

   - Redundancy and failover mechanisms
   - Cyber-informed engineering and safety integration
   - Coordinated incident response plans involving both IT and OT teams

CHAPTER 3   CHALLENGES AND CYBERSECURITY ATTACKS IN OPERATIONAL TECHNOLOGY (OT) AND INDUSTRIAL CONTROL SYSTEMS (ICS)

Summary

Today, cybersecurity incidents in ICS are considered a significant risk, with attacks becoming more frequent, sophisticated, and targeted. Governments, industries, and cybersecurity agencies now prioritize protecting these critical systems to prevent economic, environmental, and safety hazards.

In this chapter, we focused on the vulnerabilities that make ICS susceptible to attacks and the multifaceted challenges organizations face in safeguarding these crucial systems—highlighting the urgent need for comprehensive security strategies tailored to the unique demands of ICS environments.

We introduced why the ICS environment is considered challenging for security, maintenance, and operational stability and what are the factors that contribute to the difficulty of managing and safeguarding ICS including, for instance, legacy Systems and Obsolete Technology, High Availability and Reliability Requirements, etc.

Finally, examples about known ICS cybersecurity attacks were also provided.

CHAPTER 4

Operational Technology (OT) and Industrial Control Systems (ICS) Tools, Standards and Frameworks

Unlike traditional IT, ICS and OT environments have unique security requirements. They must prioritize availability, reliability, and safety over the confidentiality of data—a reverse of typical IT priorities. System downtime can result in catastrophic consequences, from operational disruptions to public safety hazards.

Additionally, many ICS components are legacy systems, architected in an era before cybersecurity threats became prominent. These older systems often lack intrinsic security features, making them vulnerable to targeted attacks from threat actors ranging from state-sponsored groups to opportunistic hackers.

CHAPTER 4 OPERATIONAL TECHNOLOGY (OT) AND INDUSTRIAL CONTROL SYSTEMS (ICS) TOOLS, STANDARDS AND FRAMEWORKS

Recent years have witnessed significant cyber incidents targeting ICS—such as ransomware attacks on energy grids or sophisticated breaches in water treatment facilities—highlighting the urgent need for robust security frameworks and tools tailored to these environments.

Attackers exploit vulnerabilities through phishing, malware, and sophisticated techniques like supply chain attacks or zero-day exploits. The integration of IoT devices further amplifies vulnerabilities, creating multiple attack vectors.

As industrial environments continue to integrate digital technologies, the focus on ICS and OT cybersecurity will intensify. Emerging technologies like AI and machine learning offer promising solutions for predictive threat detection and adaptive security measures. The adoption of Zero Trust Architecture within ICS environments is also expected to grow, fostering an "assume-breach" mindset that bolsters defense mechanisms.

Concurrently, regulatory bodies are likely to impose stricter compliance standards, compelling organizations to align with best practices and invest in their cybersecurity infrastructure.

The synergy of advanced tools, robust frameworks, and adherence to standards and regulations is crucial in securing industrial environments against present and future threats. By adopting holistic security strategies, industries can protect their critical infrastructure, ensuring reliability, safety, and operational integrity.

This chapter dives into the most important ICS/OT Security Tools, Standards, and Frameworks considering regulations and directives, which must be fulfilled these days. We will also introduce the Perdue model PERA 2.0, CIS controls and most important regulations and directives for ICS/OT.

CHAPTER 4   OPERATIONAL TECHNOLOGY (OT) AND INDUSTRIAL CONTROL SYSTEMS (ICS) TOOLS, STANDARDS AND FRAMEWORKS

Security Tools for ICS/OT

ICS and OT environments require **specialized tools** that prioritize **availability, safety, and reliability**, while still addressing modern cyber threats. A layered approach using **passive monitoring**, **secure access**, and **compliance management** is critical to building a resilient industrial cybersecurity posture.

To mitigate ICS/OT challenges, organizations rely on a range of ICS/OT-specific security tools which might include the following:

- **Anomaly Detection Systems**: Tools like intrusion detection systems (IDS) and intrusion prevention systems (IPS) that monitor network traffic for unusual patterns indicative of potential threats.

- **Endpoint Security Solutions**: Designed for legacy equipment, these solutions protect hardware with limited processing capabilities.

- **Firewalls and Network Segmentation**: Essential for isolating ICS components from potentially threatening external networks.

- **Access Management Solutions**: Tools like Privileged Access Management (PAM) restrict and monitor administrative access to critical systems.

- **Threat Intelligence Platforms**: Provide real-time insights into potential threats specific to industrial environments.

CHAPTER 4 OPERATIONAL TECHNOLOGY (OT) AND INDUSTRIAL CONTROL SYSTEMS (ICS) TOOLS, STANDARDS AND FRAMEWORKS

Here is the list of the most commonly used ICS and OT Cybersecurity Tools:

1. **Network Monitoring and Intrusion Detection Systems (IDS):**

   These tools passively monitor traffic within OT networks to detect anomalies or known attack patterns without disrupting operations.

   - **Nozomi Networks Guardian**
   - **Dragos Platform**
   - **Radiflow CIARA**
   - **SecurityMatters SilentDefense (now part of Forescout)**

   Features:

   - Protocol-aware detection (Modbus, DNP3, BACnet, etc.)
   - Passive asset discovery
   - Behavioral anomaly detection
   - Integration with SIEMs

2. **Asset Discovery and Inventory Management:**

   Visibility is foundational. These tools automatically discover and profile OT/ICS devices and communication flows:

   - **Honeywell**
   - **Forescout**
   - **Armis**

CHAPTER 4   OPERATIONAL TECHNOLOGY (OT) AND INDUSTRIAL CONTROL SYSTEMS (ICS) TOOLS, STANDARDS AND FRAMEWORKS

- **Tenable.ot**
- **Cisco Cyber Vision**

Features:

- Real-time asset inventory
- Device classification (PLCs, RTUs, HMIs, etc.)
- Network topology mapping
- Risk scoring

3. **Firewalls and Network Segmentation:**

Firewalls in OT environments often include industrial protocol support and deep packet inspection.

- **Palo Alto Networks (with OT-specific filters)**
- **Fortinet FortiGate Rugged Series**
- **Check Point Industrial Security Gateway**
- **Cisco Industrial Security Appliances**

Features:

- Zone-based segmentation (IT/OT separation)
- Industrial protocol filtering
- Secure remote access (VPNs)
- High availability for continuous uptime

4. **Configuration and Patch Management:**

These tools help manage and harden system configurations and address vulnerabilities in legacy systems.

- **Tripwire Industrial Visibility**
- **Tenable Nessus (with ICS plugins)**
- **Ivanti Neurons for OT**

Features:

- Configuration baseline monitoring
- Patch availability tracking
- Remediation planning for legacy ICS components

5. **Endpoint Detection and Response (EDR) for OT:**

   Though traditional EDR tools may not be suitable, some are tailored for OT endpoints.

   - **CyberX (acquired by Microsoft, now Defender for IoT)**
   - **Kaspersky Industrial CyberSecurity**
   - **Symantec ICS Protection**

   Features:

   - Lightweight agents or agentless monitoring
   - Behavior analysis
   - Compatibility with embedded/legacy systems

6. **Security Information and Event Management (SIEM):**

   These platforms aggregate logs from across OT and IT environments for centralized threat detection.

   - **Splunk (with OT/ICS integrations)**
   - **IBM QRadar**

CHAPTER 4　OPERATIONAL TECHNOLOGY (OT) AND INDUSTRIAL CONTROL SYSTEMS (ICS) TOOLS, STANDARDS AND FRAMEWORKS

- **LogRhythm**
- **Securonix (SIEM for Critical Infrastructure)**

Features:

- Correlation rules for ICS alerts
- Integration with OT IDS tools
- Compliance reporting

7. **Governance, Risk, and Compliance (GRC) Tools:**

Used to manage policy enforcement, audits, and regulatory alignment.

- **RSA Archer**
- **ServiceNow GRC**
- **NIST CSF and ISA/IEC 62443 compliance modules**

Features:

- Risk scoring and mitigation planning
- Framework mapping (NIS2, NERC CIP, etc.)
- Workflow automation for policy management

8. **Secure Remote Access Solutions:**

Remote maintenance is necessary—but must be secured with tools that offer granular control.

- **SSH Communications Security (PrivX OT and NQX)**
- **Dispel**
- **Cyolo**

CHAPTER 4   OPERATIONAL TECHNOLOGY (OT) AND INDUSTRIAL CONTROL SYSTEMS (ICS) TOOLS, STANDARDS AND FRAMEWORKS

- **Tenable.ot Secure Remote Access**
- **Xage Security**

Features:

- Just in Time (JIT) Access
- Identity-based access
- Session recording and approval workflows
- Protocol tunneling (RDP, SSH, etc.)

When Do We Need to Use a PAM (Privileged Access Management) Solution in an OT (Operational Technology) Environment?

A PAM (Privileged Access Management) solution is needed in an OT (Operational Technology) environment when there is a need to securely manage and control access to critical systems, devices, and infrastructure with elevated privileges—such as industrial control systems, SCADA systems, or PLCs—to prevent unauthorized access, reduce the risk of insider threats, and ensure safety and compliance during maintenance, troubleshooting, or emergency situations.

Here is an example for OT-focused PAM vendor for both IT and OT, using solution offered by **SSH Communications Security**, which is one of the companies known for providing a modern, secure, and scalable PAM solution for converging IT–OT data and systems. The solution is named **PrivX OT PAM**, which is a secure access management solution for industrial automation and manufacturing businesses that require access management at scale.

CHAPTER 4   OPERATIONAL TECHNOLOGY (OT) AND INDUSTRIAL CONTROL SYSTEMS (ICS)
            TOOLS, STANDARDS AND FRAMEWORKS

Major benefits of SSH PrivX OT PAM solution include the following:

- Integrates with IT/OT systems

- Industrial (remote) access to modern/legacy ICS targets in hybrid environments

- Local/remote troubleshooting and data collection

- Least-privilege and just-enough-access (not available with VPNs and firewalls)

- Grants just-in-time Zero Trust access to industrial targets

SSH PrivX offered IT–OT PAM solution is shown in Figure 4-1.

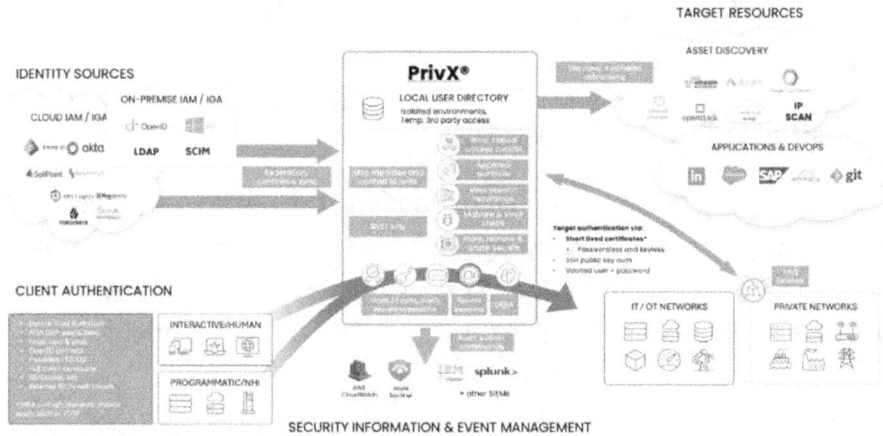

Figure 4-1. *SSH PrivX IT–OT PAM solution overview*

Figure 4-2 shows the SSH PrivX OT solution access methods such as the following:

1. Access to typical IT sources like Servers, Network devices, DBs, Applications, etc.

2. Access to OT-specific resources like PLC, HMI, etc. via Jump host Server.

105

CHAPTER 4   OPERATIONAL TECHNOLOGY (OT) AND INDUSTRIAL CONTROL SYSTEMS (ICS) TOOLS, STANDARDS AND FRAMEWORKS

3. Access to OT-specific resources such as Services, systems, or subnets which are accessed using arbitrary TCP/IP protocols.

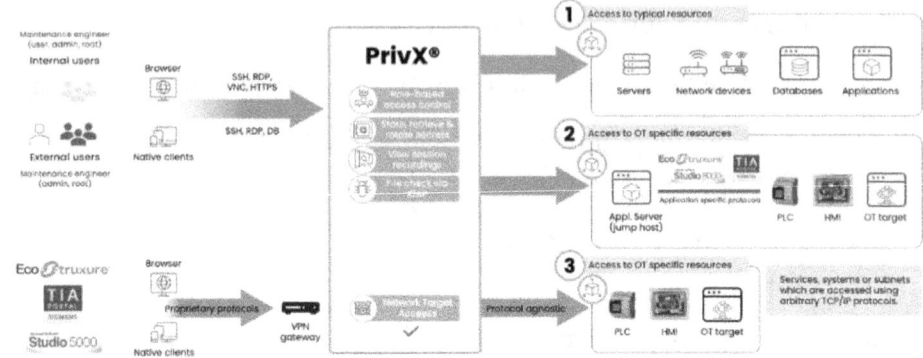

Figure 4-2. SSH PrivX OT PAM access methods

OT Security Protocols

OT security protocols focus on embedding security into every phase of operational processes, developing system resilience, and ensuring safety and reliability. They emphasize *risk management*, *defense-in-depth*, and *lifecycle security*, acknowledging the critical importance of maintaining operational continuity in industrial environments.

Table 4-1 provides a quick reference to key standards and protocols relevant to OT cybersecurity, outlining their focus and critical security aspects.

CHAPTER 4   OPERATIONAL TECHNOLOGY (OT) AND INDUSTRIAL CONTROL SYSTEMS (ICS) TOOLS, STANDARDS AND FRAMEWORKS

Table 4-1. Common OT Security Protocols

Protocol / Standard	Overview	Key Aspects	Applications/Focus
IEC 62443	International standard for ICS cybersecurity	Security levels, lifecycle management, network segmentation	Developing secure control systems
NIST SP 800-82	Guide for ICS cybersecurity best practices	Asset management, segmentation, patching, monitoring	Risk management and defensive strategies
ISA/IEC 61511 / IEC 61508	Standards for functional safety in industrial systems	Safety lifecycle, redundancy, fail-safe design	Safety-critical system security
NERC CIP	US standards for electrical utilities	Access control, incident reporting, asset monitoring	Power grid and critical infrastructure security
ISO/IEC 27001/27019	International info security management standards	Risk assessment, controls, continuous improvement	Information security in OT environments
Modbus Security	Secure version of Modbus protocol	Encryption, authentication, message integrity	Securing legacy industrial communication protocols
OPC UA Security	Built-in security features of OPC UA protocol	Authentication, encryption, message signing	Secure industrial communication

CHAPTER 4   OPERATIONAL TECHNOLOGY (OT) AND INDUSTRIAL CONTROL SYSTEMS (ICS) TOOLS, STANDARDS AND FRAMEWORKS

Figure 4-3 shows the most common Standard and Proprietary OT Systems/Protocols.

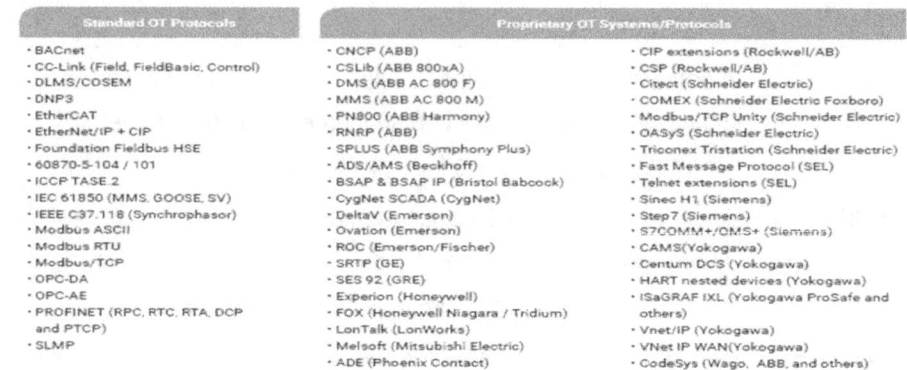

Figure 4-3. Most well-known OT protocols

OT Security Standards

Industrial Control Systems (ICS) and **Operational Technology (OT)** are the backbone of critical infrastructure sectors such as energy, water, manufacturing, transportation, and chemical processing. These systems are responsible for monitoring and controlling physical processes, often in real-time, and have traditionally operated in isolated environments.

However, as these systems become increasingly connected to enterprise IT networks and the Internet (e.g., through Industry 4.0, IIoT, and smart manufacturing), they also become more **vulnerable to cyber threats**. To address this risk, a number of international **cybersecurity standards and frameworks** have been developed specifically for ICS and OT environments.

Purpose of ICS/OT Security standards are as follows:

- Protect the **availability**, **integrity**, and **confidentiality** of industrial systems.

- Ensure the **safety of physical operations** and personnel.

- Provide **structured guidance** for risk assessment, technical controls, governance, and compliance.

- Enable organizations to build **resilient architectures** that can prevent, detect, and respond to cyber incidents.

Unlike traditional IT systems, ICS/OT systems have unique requirements:

- **High availability** and real-time operation
- **Long device lifecycles** (10–20+ years)
- **Safety-critical environments** where downtime can endanger lives
- Use of **proprietary protocols** and legacy systems that are difficult to patch
- Often **lack built-in security features**

Therefore, ICS-specific standards focus not only on cybersecurity, but also on **operational safety**, **process reliability**, and **system longevity**.

Why Do Security Standards Matter?

ICS/OT Security Standards are fundamentals because they provide

- A **common language** for IT, OT, and executive teams to align security efforts
- **Benchmarking** against global best practices

CHAPTER 4   OPERATIONAL TECHNOLOGY (OT) AND INDUSTRIAL CONTROL SYSTEMS (ICS) TOOLS, STANDARDS AND FRAMEWORKS

- Guidance for **regulatory compliance** (e.g., NIS2, NERC CIP, ISA, or sector-specific mandates)
- **Blueprints for system design**, segmentation, and defense-in-depth architecture

A full ICS/OT Cybersecurity Standards overview is shown in Table 4-2.

Table 4-2. ICS/OT Cybersecurity Standards Overview

Standard	Organization	Focus Area	Key Features
ISA/IEC 62443	ISA (International Society of Automation) / IEC	ICS/OT Cybersecurity Framework	— Comprehensive, layered security model — Defines roles for asset owners, system integrators, product suppliers — Covers risk assessment, secure design, and lifecycle management
NIST SP 800-82	NIST (US National Institute of Standards and Technology)	Guide to ICS Security	— Best practices for securing SCADA, DCS, PLCs — Integrates with broader NIST Cybersecurity Framework — Risk management tailored to industrial environments
NIST Cybersecurity Framework (CSF)	NIST	General Cybersecurity Framework for Critical Infrastructure	— Functions: Identify, Protect, Detect, Respond, Recover — Highly customizable — Widely adopted across sectors including energy and manufacturing

(continued)

CHAPTER 4   OPERATIONAL TECHNOLOGY (OT) AND INDUSTRIAL CONTROL SYSTEMS (ICS) TOOLS, STANDARDS AND FRAMEWORKS

Table 4-2. (*continued*)

Standard	Organization	Focus Area	Key Features
NERC CIP	NERC (North American Electric Reliability Corporation)	Critical Infrastructure Protection (Electric Sector)	— Mandatory for US electric utilities — Focuses on protecting bulk electric systems — Covers access control, incident response, recovery planning
ISO/IEC 27001 / 27019	ISO / IEC	Information Security Management (27019 tailored for energy)	— Information security risk management — 27019 expands to address power generation, transmission, and distribution — Aligns with ISO 9001/14001 structures
OG86 (UK)	OGUK (Oil & Gas UK)	Cybersecurity for Offshore Oil & Gas	— Specific to North Sea oil and gas operations — Integrates ICS cybersecurity with safety systems — Addresses vendor and third-party risks
TSA Pipeline Security Guidelines	TSA (US Transportation Security Administration)	Pipeline Cybersecurity	— Applies to natural gas and hazardous liquid pipelines — Includes voluntary and directive-based controls — Updated post-Colonial Pipeline attack

(*continued*)

Table 4-2. (*continued*)

Standard	Organization	Focus Area	Key Features
MITRE ATT&CK for ICS	MITRE	Threat Modeling and Intelligence	— Taxonomy of adversary tactics/techniques — Focused on ICS-specific threats — Supports threat hunting, red teaming, and incident response
ENISA Guidelines	ENISA (EU Agency for Cybersecurity)	OT & ICS Cybersecurity (EU Focus)	— Guidance for operators of essential services (under NIS Directive) — Supports cross-border cooperation and harmonization — Often used alongside IEC 62443

ICS/OT Standards should be used and combined as following:

- **Critical Infrastructure Operators** often use a **combination** of these standards (e.g., NIST CSF + IEC 62443 + MITRE ATT&CK).

- **Compliance-driven industries** (like energy and transportation) are **mandated** to follow sector-specific standards such as **NERC CIP** or **TSA directives**.

CHAPTER 4   OPERATIONAL TECHNOLOGY (OT) AND INDUSTRIAL CONTROL SYSTEMS (ICS) TOOLS, STANDARDS AND FRAMEWORKS

Here is how the ICS/OT Standards are defined based on framework:

- **IEC 62443 Series: Industrial communication networks—Network and system security**

  - IEC 62443 is a comprehensive series of standards developed by the International Electrotechnical Commission (IEC) specifically for industrial automation and control systems (IACS) security.

  - It provides a framework for implementing cybersecurity measures tailored to the unique requirements of industrial environments.

- **NIST SP 800-82 Rev. 2: Guide to Industrial Control Systems (ICS) Security**

  - Published by the National Institute of Standards and Technology (NIST), this guide focuses on securing industrial control systems.

  - It provides recommendations for managing risk, protecting against cyber threats, and improving the overall security posture of ICS.

- **ISO/IEC 27001: Information Security Management System (ISMS)**

  - ISO/IEC 27001 is a widely recognized standard for information security management.

  - While not specific to OT, organizations can use it as a foundation for developing a comprehensive security management system, including OT security.

- **ISA/IEC 62443-3-3: Security for industrial automation and control systems—Part 3-3, System security requirements and security levels**
    - This standard, part of the IEC 62443 series, focuses on defining security requirements and security levels for industrial automation and control systems.
- **ISA/IEC 62443-4-1: Security for industrial automation and control systems—Part 4-1, Secure product development lifecycle requirements**
    - Another part of the IEC 62443 series, this standard outlines secure development practices for industrial automation and control system products.
- **NIST Cybersecurity Framework (CSF):**
    - While not specific to OT, the NIST CSF provides a flexible framework that can be adapted to assess and improve cybersecurity practices across various sectors, including critical infrastructure.
- **NERC CIP (Critical Infrastructure Protection) Standards:**
    - Developed by the North American Electric Reliability Corporation (NERC), these standards focus on the security of the electricity grid.
    - NERC CIP standards include requirements for securing cyber assets, managing access, and implementing incident response measures.

CHAPTER 4   OPERATIONAL TECHNOLOGY (OT) AND INDUSTRIAL CONTROL SYSTEMS (ICS) TOOLS, STANDARDS AND FRAMEWORKS

- **API RP 1164, Pipeline SCADA Security:**

  - Developed by the American Petroleum Institute (API), this recommended practice provides guidance on security considerations for supervisory control and data acquisition (SCADA) systems in pipeline operations.

ICS and OT Security Frameworks

In the rapidly evolving landscape of industrial operations, where efficiency and connectivity are paramount, the security of Industrial Control Systems (ICS) and Operational Technology (OT) has become a pressing priority.

These systems form the backbone of critical infrastructure across industries such as energy, manufacturing, and transportation. As these environments become more interconnected, they present unique security challenges that traditional IT security measures are ill-equipped to handle.

As industries continue to adopt digital technologies, there is a growing need for adaptive and resilient security practices. Emerging technologies like AI and machine learning are being integrated into these frameworks, offering promising solutions for predictive threat detection and automated responses. Additionally, frameworks are evolving to incorporate Zero Trust principles, enhancing defense mechanisms in the face of evolving threats.

In conclusion, ICS and OT security frameworks are essential for guiding industries in protecting their critical infrastructure. They offer a roadmap to navigate the complexities of industrial cybersecurity, ensuring reliability, safety, and operational integrity in an increasingly interconnected world.

CHAPTER 4   OPERATIONAL TECHNOLOGY (OT) AND INDUSTRIAL CONTROL SYSTEMS (ICS) TOOLS, STANDARDS AND FRAMEWORKS

ICS/OT Key Frameworks include the following:

- **IEC 62443:** Offers comprehensive guidelines for securing industrial automation and control systems, focusing on lifecycle security and risk management.

- **NIST SP 800-82:** Provides best practices for integrating cybersecurity into industrial control systems, emphasizing asset management and monitoring.

- **NERC CIP:** Focuses on safeguarding the North American bulk electric system, mandating strict compliance standards for utilities.

- **ISO/IEC 27001:** An information security management standard that, when applied to OT, emphasizes risk-based control implementation.

Also to consider

- **NIST SP 800-53**
- **NIST SP 800-171**
- **NIST Cybersecurity Framework**
- **NIST SP 1800 Series**
- **HITRUST Common Security Framework (HITRUST CSF)**
- **ENISA**
- **COBIT**
- **OWASP**

CHAPTER 4   OPERATIONAL TECHNOLOGY (OT) AND INDUSTRIAL CONTROL SYSTEMS (ICS) TOOLS, STANDARDS AND FRAMEWORKS

Introduction of Standards and Technology (NIST) Cybersecurity Framework (CSF)

In an era where digital transformation is revolutionizing industries, safeguarding critical infrastructure has become more crucial than ever. The **NIST Cybersecurity Framework (CSF)** provides organizations with a flexible, risk-based approach to managing and reducing cybersecurity risks across all sectors, including industrial control systems (ICS) and operational technology (OT).

Developed by the National Institute of Standards and Technology (NIST), the CSF was initially published in 2014 in response to executive order 13636, aimed at improving the cybersecurity of critical infrastructure in the United States. It has since become a globally recognized standard, adopted by organizations worldwide regardless of size or sector.

The framework is composed of **five key functions** that provide a high-level, strategic view of cybersecurity management:

- **Identify:** Understand organizational assets, data, risks, and vulnerabilities.

- **Protect:** Implement safeguards to ensure delivery of critical services.

- **Detect:** Develop activities to identify cybersecurity events promptly.

- **Respond:** Take action against detected anomalies to contain impact.

- **Recover:** Plan and implement procedures to restore operations after an incident.

CHAPTER 4 OPERATIONAL TECHNOLOGY (OT) AND INDUSTRIAL CONTROL SYSTEMS (ICS) TOOLS, STANDARDS AND FRAMEWORKS

Key Features include the following:

- **Risk-Based and Flexible:** Organizations can tailor the framework based on their specific risks, resources, and operational environment.

- **Aligned with Standards and Best Practices:** It incorporates existing standards like ISO, IEC, and NIST SP 800-53.

- **Prioritized Approach:** Focuses on critical assets and activities to optimize resource allocation.

- **Continuous Improvement:** Emphasizes ongoing assessment and refinement of cybersecurity practices.

NIST CFS key benefits are as follows:

- Enhances organizational resilience by providing a common language for communication.

- Facilitates regulatory compliance and stakeholder confidence.

- Improves incidents response and recovery capabilities.

- Supports integration with existing risk management processes.

The NIST CSF is a valuable tool for organizations seeking to develop a proactive, comprehensive cybersecurity posture. Its adaptable structure helps organizations of all sizes and sectors to better understand their cybersecurity risks, prioritize resources, and strengthen defenses—especially vital for securing critical infrastructure and ICS/OT environments.

CHAPTER 4   OPERATIONAL TECHNOLOGY (OT) AND INDUSTRIAL CONTROL SYSTEMS (ICS) TOOLS, STANDARDS AND FRAMEWORKS

The objective is to undertake a cyber risk assessment of the client's operational plants in line with the NIST Cybersecurity Framework to identify the actions required to meet target maturity across the five dimensions of Identify, Protect, Detect, Respond and Recover.

Commonly used Security assessment methodology is as follows:

- **NIST CS Framework** through a series of workshops and interviews, together with desk-based research, to review cybersecurity capabilities and maturity status. Comprehensive cybersecurity assessment and OT asset discovery and remediation plan across client's manufacturing sites.

- **NIST CSF** will be used to review critical systems in place at each site to identify those requiring remediation, utilizing all available local resources including security tools (as available), site artefacts, and remote work sessions with site SMEs.

Figure 4-4 shows the NIST Cybersecurity Framework.

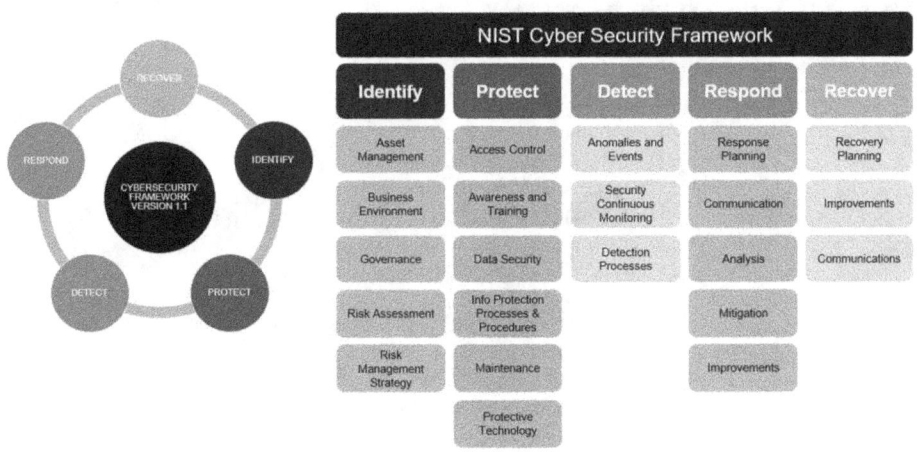

Figure 4-4. *NIST Cybersecurity framework*

CHAPTER 4   OPERATIONAL TECHNOLOGY (OT) AND INDUSTRIAL CONTROL SYSTEMS (ICS)
TOOLS, STANDARDS AND FRAMEWORKS

Figure 4-5 shows the OT Cybersecurity Framework based on NIST CSF.

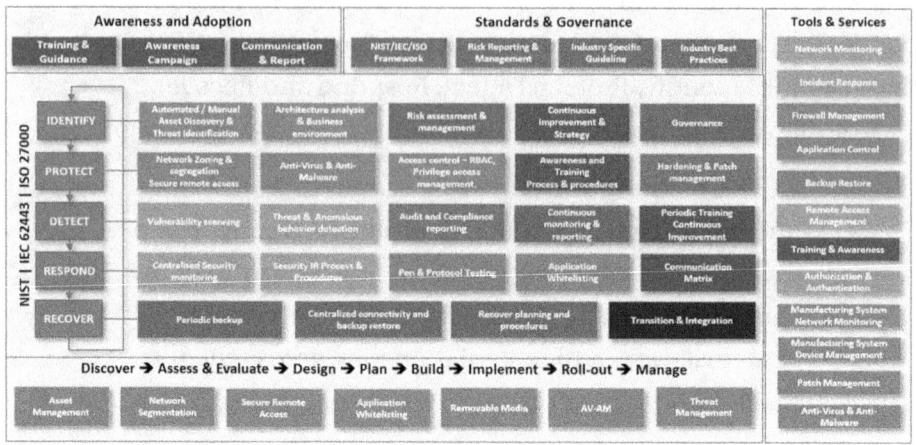

Figure 4-5. *OT Cybersecurity Framework based on NIST CSF*

Figure 4-6 shows OT Security Framework as a combination of standards like ISA/IEC 62443 and NIST.

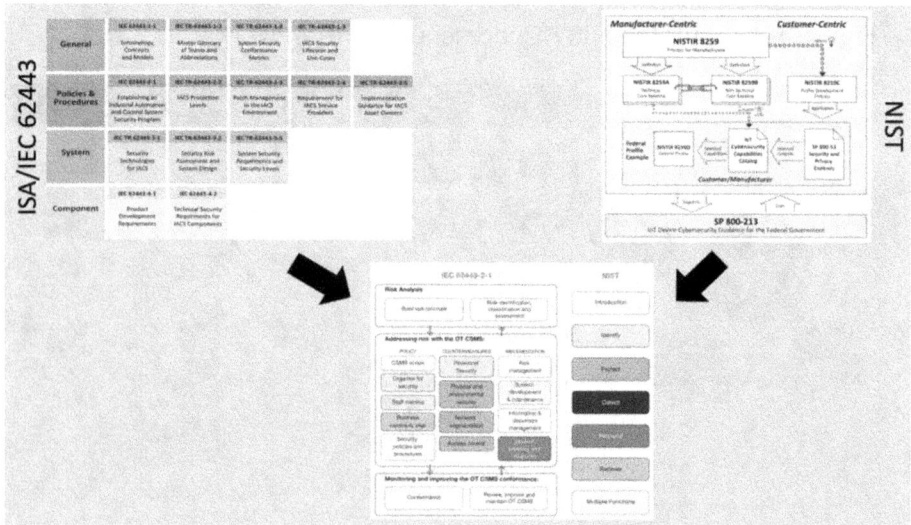

Figure 4-6. *OT Security Framework as a combination of standards*

CHAPTER 4   OPERATIONAL TECHNOLOGY (OT) AND INDUSTRIAL CONTROL SYSTEMS (ICS) TOOLS, STANDARDS AND FRAMEWORKS

Purdue Enterprise Reference Architecture (PERA) 2.0

Traditionally, OT networks have adopted various Models, Architectures, and Systems to secure the OT Infrastructure. An example is the Purdue Model for Control Hierarchy.

The Purdue Enterprise Reference Architecture was created in the mid-1990s and quickly found broad industry acceptance as a means to understand the required hierarchical structure of OT systems. It is incorporated into the ANSI/ISA-95 standard, which maps the interconnections and interdependencies of the high-level components of a typical industrial control system (ICS).

The Purdue model, also known as **PERA 2.0,** is an evolved framework that provides a comprehensive, layered architecture for industrial automation, control, and enterprise systems. It guides organizations in designing secure, reliable, and scalable industrial control environments by offering a reference model that aligns business, control, and manufacturing operations.

The main purpose of PERA 2.0 is to establish a standardized blueprint for integrating enterprise-level systems with control systems, ensuring seamless data flow, security, and system interoperability.

- **Core Focus:**
  - Segmentation of enterprise, control, and manufacturing layers.
  - Incorporation of security best practices.
  - Enhancing interoperability among diverse systems and vendors.

CHAPTER 4   OPERATIONAL TECHNOLOGY (OT) AND INDUSTRIAL CONTROL SYSTEMS (ICS) TOOLS, STANDARDS AND FRAMEWORKS

- **Updates in 2.0:**

  - Emphasizes cybersecurity and resiliency.

  - Incorporates modern industrial technologies like IoT.

  - Addresses the challenges of Industry 4.0, including cloud integration and big data analytics.

Key Benefits are as follows:

- Provides a common language and structure for system design.

- Facilitates security by design across all layers.

- Enhances flexibility for future technological expansion.

The Purdue Model for Control Hierarchy is a common and well understood model in the manufacturing industry that provides a Blueprint to segments Devices and Equipment into hierarchical functions. It includes the layers shown in Table 4-3.

CHAPTER 4   OPERATIONAL TECHNOLOGY (OT) AND INDUSTRIAL CONTROL SYSTEMS (ICS) TOOLS, STANDARDS AND FRAMEWORKS

Table 4-3. *Layers of the Purdue Model*

Layer	Description	Typical Components	Security Focus
Level 4 – Enterprise	Business planning and logistics	ERP, business management systems	Protecting business data, policies, and external communication
Level 3 – Site Business/ Operations	Operations management	Manufacturing Execution Systems (MES), production schedules	Secure information flow between business and control processes
Level 2 – Site Control	Supervisory control	SCADA, HMI, Historian systems	Control system safety, real-time monitoring
Level 1 – Control	Basic Control; PLCs, RTUs	PLCs, controllers, sensors	Physical device security, process integrity
Level 0 – Physical Process	Sensors, actuators	Field devices, sensors, actuators	Physical process safety and security

Here is an explanation of the PERA layers:

- **Level 4—Enterprise:**

    1. **Description:** Manages business-related applications and functions such as ERP, financial management, and logistics.

    2. **Focus:** Business planning and logistics.

- **Level 3—Operations Management:**

    1. **Description:** Coordinates site-wide operations and production activities using systems like MES (Manufacturing Execution Systems).

    2. **Focus:** Operations management and workflow optimization.

- **Level 2—Supervisory Control:**

    1. **Description:** Oversees supervisory functions including SCADA and HMI systems for monitoring and control.

    2. **Focus:** Real-time monitoring and process visualization.

- **Level 1—Control:**

    1. **Description:** Includes control systems such as PLCs and RTUs that directly manage production processes.

    2. **Focus:** Automated control of manufacturing processes.

- **Level 0—Process:**

    1. **Description:** Encompasses physical devices such as sensors and actuators that interface with the actual production process.

    2. **Focus:** Direct interaction with machinery and physical processes.

Figures 4-7 and 4-8 show a highlight vision of PERA 2.0 and a detailed architecture overview.

CHAPTER 4   OPERATIONAL TECHNOLOGY (OT) AND INDUSTRIAL CONTROL SYSTEMS (ICS) TOOLS, STANDARDS AND FRAMEWORKS

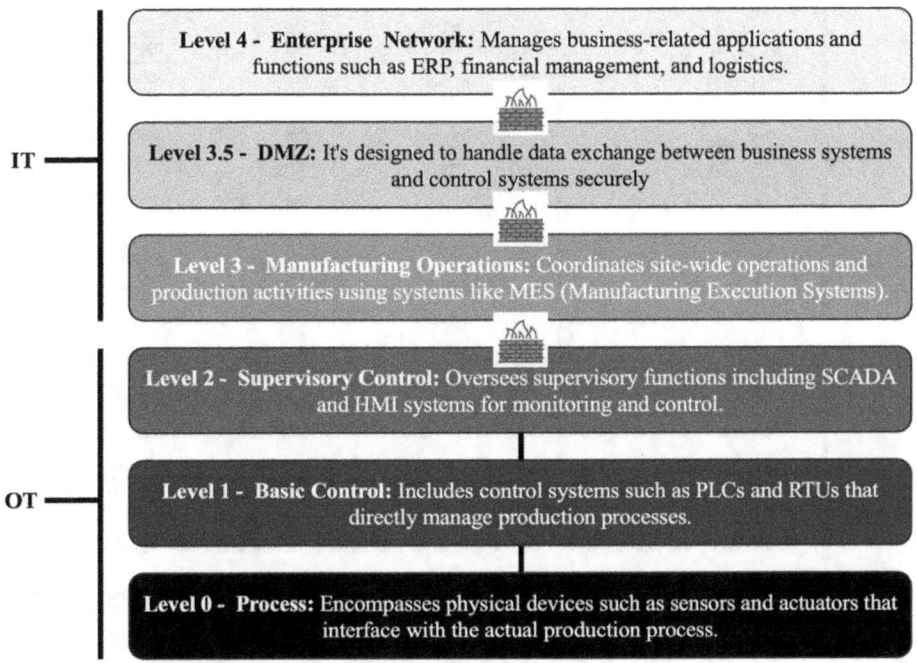

Figure 4-7. PERA 2.0 overview

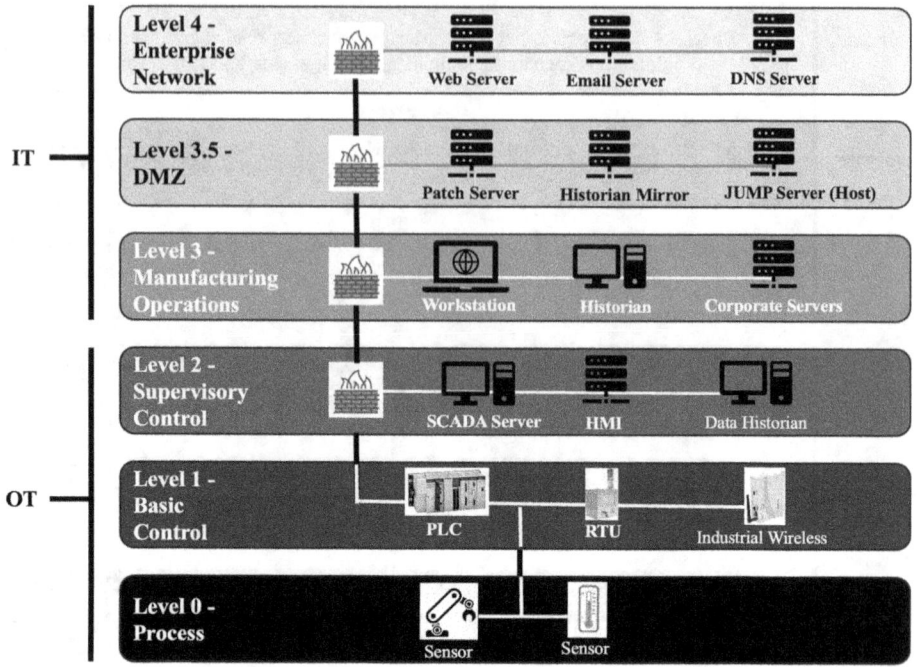

Figure 4-8. Detailed PERA 2.0 overview

The Purdue Model remains a fundamental blueprint for secure industrial architectures, facilitating a systematic approach to segmentation, security, and interoperability in industrial networks. Its layered structure helps organizations reduce vulnerabilities, improve resilience, and comply with industry standards.

ICS and OT Security Regulations and Directives

Compliance with these regulations and standards is crucial for organizations managing ICS and OT environments. They provide a structured approach to risk management, security controls, safety integration, and incident response. Implementing these directives helps reduce vulnerability, ensure operational resilience, and meet legal and contractual obligations.

Modern OT environments—particularly those operating in **critical infrastructure sectors** (energy, water, transport, manufacturing, etc.)—are increasingly subject to **cybersecurity laws, regulations, and directives**. These are designed to improve **resilience**, **incident response**, and **risk management** in the face of growing cyber threats.

Why Regulations and Directives Matter for OT Security?

- **Legal obligations**: Non-compliance can result in fines, shutdowns, or contract loss.
- **Operational alignment**: These laws promote cybersecurity **without compromising availability and safety**.
- **Incident accountability**: Mandatory **incident reporting** ensures quicker national or sectoral response to cyberattacks.
- **Supply chain influence**: Large industrial organizations require compliance from vendors and integrators.

Table 4-4 provides a list of the key OT Security regulations and directives.

CHAPTER 4   OPERATIONAL TECHNOLOGY (OT) AND INDUSTRIAL CONTROL SYSTEMS (ICS)
TOOLS, STANDARDS AND FRAMEWORKS

Table 4-4. Most Common OT Security Regulations and Directives

Regulation/ Directive	Applies to	Purpose	Key OT Impact
NIS2 Directive *(EU)*	Operators of essential services and critical infrastructure	Enhances EU-wide cyber resilience and incident reporting	Mandatory risk management, incident reporting, supply chain security, enforced at national level
GDPR *(EU)*	Any entity processing personal data of EU citizens	Protects privacy and data handling	OT systems that collect or store personal data (e.g., smart grids, building controls) must comply
NERC CIP *(North America)*	Bulk electric system operators	Ensures cyber and physical security of power grids	Requires technical, procedural, and policy controls; applies directly to industrial systems
HIPAA *(USA)*	Healthcare providers and their systems	Protects patient health data	If OT systems (e.g., building automation in hospitals) touch PHI, they must comply
Cybersecurity Maturity Model Certification (CMMC) *(USA)*	Defense contractors & supply chain	Secures Controlled Unclassified Information (CUI)	OT used in manufacturing or logistics may need to meet DoD cybersecurity requirements

(continued)

CHAPTER 4   OPERATIONAL TECHNOLOGY (OT) AND INDUSTRIAL CONTROL SYSTEMS (ICS) TOOLS, STANDARDS AND FRAMEWORKS

Table 4-4. (*continued*)

Regulation/ Directive	Applies to	Purpose	Key OT Impact
ISA/IEC 62443 *(Global)*	ICS/OT asset owners, integrators, vendors	Provides a standards-based framework for OT cybersecurity	Widely adopted voluntarily or mandated by regulators in critical infrastructure
NIST SP 800-82 / 800-53 *(USA)*	Federal agencies, contractors	Guides for securing ICS and control systems	Used as baseline in government and regulated industries
Critical Infrastructure Protection Act *(Various countries)*	National-level operators	Protects national infrastructure from cyber-physical threats	Encourages risk assessments, protective measures, and reporting
UK NIS Regulations *(UK)*	Operators of essential services	UK's version of NIS post-Brexit	Requires secure OT environments and reporting of significant cyber incidents
BDEW Whitepaper *(Germany)*	Energy sector organizations	Security framework for German energy systems	Covers risk management, network segmentation, and secure remote access

CHAPTER 4   OPERATIONAL TECHNOLOGY (OT) AND INDUSTRIAL CONTROL SYSTEMS (ICS) TOOLS, STANDARDS AND FRAMEWORKS

How to Integrate Regulations and Directives?

- Align your **OT cybersecurity program** with both **technical standards** (e.g., IEC 62443) and **regulatory frameworks** (e.g., NIS2).

- Implement **risk-based segmentation, multi-factor authentication, secure remote access**, and **event monitoring** as universal compliance actions.

- Use **governance structures** (CISO, security policies, training) to meet both IT and OT compliance needs.

Center Internet Security (CIS) 20 for ICS and OT

The **CIS 20**—also known as the CIS Critical Security Controls v7.1—is a prioritized set of 20 cybersecurity best practices developed by the **Center for Internet Security (CIS)**. These controls were designed to help organizations defend against the most common and impactful cyber threats, primarily in traditional IT environments. However, many of these principles can be adapted to secure ICS (Industrial Control Systems) and OT (Operational Technology).

The generic set of Center Internet Security (CIS) 20 Controls provide a good baseline for cybersecurity and can be tailored to OT environments. The most used controls, grouped into Basic, Foundational, and Organizational categories, are listed here:

- **CIS Control #1: Inventory and Control of Hardware Assets**

CHAPTER 4   OPERATIONAL TECHNOLOGY (OT) AND INDUSTRIAL CONTROL SYSTEMS (ICS) TOOLS, STANDARDS AND FRAMEWORKS

- **CIS Control #2: Inventory and Control of Software Assets**
- **CIS Control #3: Continuous Vulnerability Assessment and Remediation**
- **CIS Control #4: Controlled Use of Administrative Privileges**
- **CIS Control #5: Secure Configuration for Hardware and Software on Mobile Devices, Laptops, Workstations and Servers**
- **CIS Control #6: Maintenance, Monitoring, and Analysis of Audit Logs**
- **CIS Control #7: Email and Web Browser Protections**
- **CIS Control #8: Malware Defenses**
- **CIS Control #9: Limitation and Control of Network Ports, Protocols, and Services**
- **CIS Control #10: Data Recovery Capability**
- **CIS Control #11: Secure Configuration for Network Devices**
- **CIS Control #12: Boundary Defense**
- **CIS Control #13: Data Protection**
- **CIS Control #14: Controlled Access**
- **CIS Control #15: Wireless Access Control**
- **CIS Control #16: Account Monitoring and Control**
- **CIS Control #17: Security Skills Assessment and Training**
- **CIS Control #18: Application Software Security**

CHAPTER 4   OPERATIONAL TECHNOLOGY (OT) AND INDUSTRIAL CONTROL SYSTEMS (ICS) TOOLS, STANDARDS AND FRAMEWORKS

- **CIS Control #19: Incident Response and Management**
- **CIS Control #20: Penetration Tests and Red Team Exercises**

Critical Security Controls for ICS and OT

The **Critical Security Controls** for **Industrial Control Systems (ICS)** and **Operational Technology (OT)** are essential measures that help protect industrial environments from cyber threats, ensuring **availability**, **integrity**, and **safety**. These controls are often adapted from general cybersecurity frameworks (like NIST, CIS, and IEC 62443) and customized for the unique needs of ICS/OT networks.

1. **Asset Inventory and Network Visibility**
2. **Network Segmentation and Boundary Defense**
3. **Access Control and Identity Management**
4. **Secure Configuration and Hardening**
5. **Continuous Monitoring and Intrusion Detection**
6. **Patch and Vulnerability Management**
7. **Data Protection and Integrity**
8. **Incident Response and Recovery**
9. **Supply Chain and Third-Party Risk Management**
10. **Security Awareness and Training**

Table 4-5 shows how to map security controls to Standards.

CHAPTER 4 OPERATIONAL TECHNOLOGY (OT) AND INDUSTRIAL CONTROL SYSTEMS (ICS) TOOLS, STANDARDS AND FRAMEWORKS

Table 4-5. Mapping Security Controls to Standards

Control Area	NIST SP 800-82	IEC 62443	CIS Controls
Asset Inventory	Yes	2-1, 3-3	#1
Access Control	Yes	3-3	#6
Network Segmentation	Yes	3-3, 3-1	#14
Monitoring	Yes	3-2, 3-3	#8
Patch Management	Yes	2-4	#7
Incident Response	Yes	2-4	#17

Summary

ICS and OT environments have unique security needs that prioritize availability, reliability, and safety over data confidentiality, making them vulnerable to legacy system vulnerabilities, cyberattacks, and increasingly complex threat vectors, especially with IoT integration.

In this chapter, we emphasized how the recent incidents highlight the urgent need for tailored security frameworks, and especially we described how emerging technologies like AI, machine learning, and Zero Trust Architecture can enhance defense capabilities.

We focused on explaining how strong regulations and standards are essential, and adopting comprehensive security tools, frameworks, and models like PERA 2.0 and CIS controls will be vital to protecting critical infrastructure now and in the future.

GPSR Compliance
The European Union's (EU) General Product Safety Regulation (GPSR) is a set of rules that requires consumer products to be safe and our obligations to ensure this.

If you have any concerns about our products, you can contact us on

ProductSafety@springernature.com

In case Publisher is established outside the EU, the EU authorized representative is:

Springer Nature Customer Service Center GmbH
Europaplatz 3
69115 Heidelberg, Germany

www.ingramcontent.com/pod-product-compliance
Lightning Source LLC
LaVergne TN
LVHW020413070526
838199LV00054B/3600